the dating game

JO HEMMINGS

NEW HOLLAND

First published in 2003 by
New Holland Publishers (UK) Ltd
London • Cape Town • Sydney • Auckland

www.newhollandpublishers.com

Garfield House
86–88 Edgware Road
London W2 2EA
United Kingdom

80 McKenzie Street
Cape Town 8001
South Africa

14 Aquatic Drive
Frenchs Forest, NSW 2086
Australia

218 Lake Road
Northcote
Auckland
New Zealand

ISBN 1 84330 494-5

Editor: Deborah Taylor
Designer: Alan Marshall
Production: Lucy Hulme

Reproduction by Pica Digital (Pte) Ltd, Singapore
Printed and bound by Kyodo Printing Co (Singapore) Ltd

Photograph and artwork acknowledgements
Front cover: Alan Marshall
Author photograph by Chris Coe

Contents

ACKNOWLEDGEMENTS

It would be far too tempting to name – and in some cases shame – those men that have helped shape the backbone of this book. So, I'm just going to thank a handful of friends and colleagues who have freely given advice, suffered my dating tales with forbearance and in some cases, positive relish.

I wonder where I'd be without friends like Jo G, who's encouraged me every step of the way throughout writing this book and advised in the best possible way. Robert, for being the best chum a girl could have – handsome, funny and never judgemental over all the years we've been the closest of mates. Johnny B – for his never ending relationship complications which make my life look straightforward and Johnny W for constantly taking the piss out of me in the gentlest possible way. Ali, Pat, Bobbie, Jude, Rosemary, Sophie, Coral, Jo S, Sumi and Sandra – for all those great evenings out and always being able to laugh at life. One or two of you are lurking within these pages… To Shyama and Karen for their practical advice and good humour.

My boys, who've suffered a distracted mother for months – and whose attitudes to the research, writing and publication of *The Dating Game* have quite rightly, varied from utter indifference to total embarrassment. And to Bob – for being the most understanding ex a woman could have.

And of course to Sarah and Rachel – one of the most sorted couples I know – forever being there to provide a wonderful refuge away from the city, always keeping me grounded and for forgiving me for including scant information on gay relationships in this book.

Introduction

What does a title like *The Dating Game* say to you? That dating is fun and an end in itself rather than a means to an end? I hope so, because that is what is intended. This book is not a guide to catching and keeping your man, staying in love for the rest of your life or playing by the dreaded 'Rules' and compromising your integrity and independence at every turn just to please a man. There are plenty of those earnest volumes around already. Neither is it a flip, trivial look at dating which skims the surface and entertains but is short on practical advice. There are plenty of those around too.

Instead, I hope *The Dating Game* will be entertaining, good fun and that it will make you laugh, as well as giving you plenty of practical advice, information and some serious food for thought along the way. It's about leaving the stigma of the 'Sad Single' behind you and celebrating what you are – a 21st century, independent woman and a 'Selective Single'. Someone who knows her own mind, enjoys life to the full and doesn't have a panic attack when she hasn't got her next date lined up.

If you've got as far as buying (or borrowing) this book, then there is a good chance that you are one of the 4 million 'singletons' aged between 25 and 44 living in the UK today. You are also most likely to be a woman and so I've written this book with women in mind. But, while I don't claim or believe that men and women are alien to each other or from different planets (as some relationship gurus would have us believe), there are clear and significant differences between the sexes and the way in which we approach dating, flirting, communication, body language and a whole host of other things.

Unlike other books, which may have struggled to take in these different perspectives and tried too hard to accommodate both male and female attitudes, I have taken the more clear cut (and easier!) route of dealing with dating from a woman's view point only. That's not to say that you guys out there shouldn't read it – quite the opposite. If you want to learn a little more about what makes us girls tick, then take a closer look. You may be more than a little surprised by what's here!

For the same reasons, although I hope that the gay women (and men) amongst you will enjoy the book too and find something useful in it, I have adopted a predominantly heterosexual approach. However, there should be plenty of useful and apposite information for gays too – you just have to adapt the bits that don't apply!

So, who am I? Well, I trained as a psychologist – although that's kind of irrelevant, other than proving that I've got a more than passing interest in what goes on in other people's lives and how they behave. I'm certainly not an expert, in the purest sense of the word, and I haven't undertaken years of psycho-sexual research at some smart sounding institution or interviewed a thousand people when creating this book. I'm a woman with common sense, a smattering of knowledge and considerable interest in how relationships work, some very close girl friends and a fairly long and mixed history of dating. I've married and divorced, had some amazing relationships and a whole raft of dating 'disasters'. So possibly I'm much like many of you...

GETTING THE MOST OUT OF THIS BOOK

While *The Dating Game* is written in a roughly logical sequence, in order to enable you to dip in and out of the book at will and get the most out of whichever chapters you feel most suit you at different stages in your dating 'career', I have written this brief summary of each individual chapter.

Starting Over

Whether you're relatively new to the dating game – as a novice or someone fresh out of a long-term relationship – or a veteran dater, this chapter will help you take a look at what you want out of a relationship. For all of us, our needs and wants vary. What makes us feel good when dating or alone changes as we go through different stages in our lives. This chapter will help you to think about what you want now. Topics include:

• Meeting people

• Taking time for reflection

• The Five Golden Rules when starting a new relationship

• Having fun

• Expectations

• Sex

The Single Life

There's a significant difference between being alone and being lonely. Loneliness is a state of mind, generally resulting from a lack of intimacy or companionship, and can lead to a feeling of lack of self-worth. Being alone is a physical state where we're simply on our own, not in a current relationship and not constantly surrounded by people and activities. This chapter gives advice on how to deal with loneliness as well as emphasizing just how important periods of being alone can be for us all. Topics include:

• Fear of being lonely

• Learning to enjoy your own company

• The good things about being single

• Fifteen reasons to celebrate singledom

Expectations

We all need personal parameters and ideals when it comes to choosing a mate. These are unique to our make-up and help us to reduce the risk of dating a whole string of unsuitables. This chapter shows that it pays to learn from past experiences in order to re-evaluate our parameters and that having unrealistic expectations can hold us back when playing the dating game. Topics include:

- The perfect man

- Making your wish list

- Being realistic about yourself

- Dumped – how to spot the signs

Self-confidence and Self-esteem

Feeling good about ourselves is absolutely key to success and happiness in any relationship. The old cliché that we need to learn to love ourselves before others can love us is never more true than when we are dating. Our levels of confidence and self-esteem vary throughout our lives and while the truly shy people amongst us have a tougher time than most when dating, even the person brimming with confidence experiences self-doubt and first-date nerves. This chapter helps you to take a look at yourself, assess your own levels of self-confidence and suggests ways you can work on those areas of yourself which cause you most concern. Topics include:

- Improving your own level of self-esteem

- Giving yourself time and space

- The power of positive thinking

- Natural self-confidence

- The ten key qualities of self-confident people

- Overcoming shyness

- Dependency

- Sexual self-confidence

Communication

Communication is not just about knowing what to say and when to say it, it is also about listening and responding to people in the most effective and productive way. While some people find this as natural as breathing, most of us have problems communicating at certain times, especially when on a first date or when we're out to impress. This chapter provides some advice on getting those all-important early impressions right. Topics include:

• Effective listening

• Making an approach

• Do's and don'ts of first contact

• Are you a good communicator?

• Communication after the first date

Compatibility

What makes us compatible with someone else? What is it – beyond simply having interests or friends in common – that makes one guy so right for us while another is so obviously wrong? This chapter looks at the individual elements that make up compatibility and how you can learn to recognize the signs that will work best for you. Topics include:

• Chemistry

• Looks

• Sex appeal

• How compatible are you?

• A compatibility test

• Using star signs to assess compatibility

Venus and Mars

While there are obvious differences – emotionally and physically – between men and women, it is unhelpful for us to look at the opposite sex as aliens from another planet. We are a mixture of our upbringing and our genetic make-up: the familiar nature versus nurture argument, and we differ hugely as individuals regardless of our sex. However, there are some fundamental differences between the sexes that are worth knowing about, so that you can stay one step ahead in the dating game. Topics include:

• Dating

• The male's eye view of the first date

• The female's eye view of the first date

- The alternative 'Rules'

- Communication

- Misunderstanding body language

- Emotions

- How we cope with stress

Flirt Mode

Flirting is about both 'flirter' and 'flirtee' feeling good. It's fun, entertaining and can range from being an almost innocent pastime to being deliciously naughty. And the great news is that we can all learn to flirt with ease and find the level that feels comfortable for us. It's just another method of communication. Topics include:

- The joy of flirting

- Flirt mode or friend mode?

- Grabbing his attention

- Being a natural flirt

- Using your voice

- Learning to flirt

- Successful flirting

Body Language

Body language speaks volumes about our attitudes, behaviour and responses. Whatever we may say, if we are not being honest, our body language will give us away. Body language is made up of non-verbal gestures, postures and expressions and this chapter will give you some surprising insights into what you and your date may be really 'saying' to each other. Topics include:

- The way we communicate

- Positive body language signs

- Negative body language signs

- First, second or third date body language

- Your body language style

- Changing your body language

Dating and Sex

This can be a dating minefield as it signals that two people are in a relationship rather than just friends. Relationships can go well beyond their natural lifespan when sex is good and can come to an abrupt end if it's not. The point at which we have sex when dating always concerns us – too soon and we worry that we might be seen as 'loose', too long and we worry that he might not stick around for the finale. Whatever we choose to do, sex is a vital element in most successful relationships and this chapter takes a look at the role it plays. Topics include:

- The importance of sex
- To tease or not to tease…
- When is the right time to have sex?
- Worrying about our bodies
- The GIB factor
- Sexual performance
- Great sex the first time
- Casual sex
- Help! Our sex drives don't match
- Your sexual health

Mind the Gap

The controversy over significant age differences in relationships rumbles on. While it is still deemed acceptable for an older man to date a younger woman, it is often frowned upon or not taken seriously when it is the other way around. Yet we live in an age when the 'rules of engagement' are constantly changing and it is becoming ever more acceptable to breach the last taboo in the dating game. This chapter looks at age gaps in relationships and lays bare the pros and cons of dating either a significantly older or a significantly younger guy. Topics include:

- Toy-boys
- Sex with a younger man
- Sugar Daddies
- Sex with an older man
- Baggage and older men
- Do you want him younger or older?

Relationships

Where we meet our dating partner plays a significant role in determining what kind of relationship it turns out to be and whether it will succeed or fail. The dating scene has changed enormously in the last generation, empowering women to meet people through work, in clubs, on holiday and even in the supermarket. What are the pros and cons of these different meeting places and how can we deal with the relationships that ensue? This chapter looks at many dating scenarios and how we can handle them. Topics include:

- The office romance
- The office party
- The holiday romance
- Long-distance relationships
- Inappropriate relationships
- Second time around
- Dating on the rebound
- Bad relationships
- Matched and despatched

Love@First Site

Long gone are the days when you could meet a nice chap at the local dance, be courted, get wed and have 2.4 children, giving up your job along the way so you could keep home and rear your children. Dating has moved on in the last few years allowing women to meet men through areas as diverse as Internet dating sites, speed dating and other organized dating events. Text messaging, emails and mobile phones have also liberated us from the 'waiting-by-the-phone-to-see-if-he-rings' syndrome. Now, we have a whole raft of options available to us as a result of new technology. Topics include:

- Internet dating
- The 21st century dating agency
- Personal ads
- Dating events
- Speed dating
- Email
- Mobile phones
- Text appeal

Chapter 1

starting
over

welcome to the
dating game

Okay, so you're fresh out of a relationship, new to the dating game or simply out of practice. First, you need to consider what you actually want out of any new relationship. A little non-committal fun, a steady long-term relationship or maybe just to go with the flow and see what happens. What is so important in the dating game – and something I shall be guilty of repeating *ad nauseam* throughout this book – is that dating should be seen as an end in itself rather than simply a means to an end i.e. culminating in a long-term relationship or marriage. Dating a variety of people enables us to find out what we really want from life – what floats our boat, pops our cork and makes us happy, fulfilled people. It is only by participating in the full range of experiences that dating has to offer that we can learn to recognize the unique mix of personality, looks and background that go to make one person, above all others, so special to us as an individual.

Maybe you turned to this chapter because you are looking to start again in a new relationship after previous unhappy experiences. Maybe you don't know what you want out of a relationship, other than that you know that you do want one and that you don't want a repeat of past miserable experiences. No guarantees there of course, but you can learn from the past. That's what it's there for – to shape us into the individuals that we are today and to help us understand where we are going and what we want out of life. Dating someone new can bring you joy, huge amounts of fun and a whole wealth of new experiences. It can also bring you heartache, misery and anxiety. Without delving into introspective self-analysis or investing in Kleenex shares, you can look back on your past relationships and work out what were the really rewarding and enjoyable bits. You can then begin to bring to the table what makes you feel good, what you want from life and enjoy discovering stuff you didn't even consider possible or important in previous relationships. It's not always easy – after all, it's human nature to analyze the dying embers of a dead relationship to try and find what went wrong and how you could have made things different, and it's easy to forget that there were any good times at all!

Meeting people

Take maximum advantage of any invites that come your way, however dull they may seem. Use each occasion as practice for those flirting skills you'll learn in Chapter 8: Flirt Mode. But don't go overboard, especially with your mates' partners – you don't want to be seen as the predatory single woman on the loose – but always make sure you look good by painting your nails or wearing killer heels, whatever makes *you* feel at your best. Make eye contact, ask questions, smile, and give compliments – to both men and women.

Never underestimate how difficult it might actually be to meet a man. There are times when you'll need to be proactive. Below is a list of just some of the places that you could meet someone, but remember it could happen anywhere and at any time, however unlikely a setting it may seem...

Bars and pubs

These can be great, especially when crowded. You can take the long way around to the loo to get near a guy you've spotted, push forward to get a drink (even when it's not your round) just to get closer to a cute guy at the bar or spill your drink accidentally-on-purpose to get his attention. And if all that sounds a little too proactive for you, you can just people-watch and give a friendly smile when someone catches your eye. You can then move nearer to the object of your desire (just to get away from the really crowded bit of the bar, of course!) and get a conversation going on the flimsiest of bases. Try 'it's more crowded in here than usual' or 'excuse me, could I just squeeze past you to get to the bar?' – they are far better opening gambits than 'do you come here often?'! A device you can use to escape the crowd is to watch for when *he* goes to the loo, wait a moment or two, then make your own exit to the Ladies, just passing by him on the stairs. A smile and a moment's eye contact will give him the all-clear to move in later and avoid possible rejection.

Parties

These can be perfect meeting places. You've got every excuse to dress to the nines and look drop-dead gorgeous and there's almost always some connection between that seriously hot guy and the host or hostess, so you've got the ideal opportunity to do a little detective work before you make an approach. And just like in the pub or bar, you can simply smile and move in there with a good opening like 'how do you know the host/hostess?', 'do you live locally?' or 'what's that punch like?' (having first chucked the tell-tale contents of your own glass into the nearest plant pot, of course). Just make sure you keep a watch for any signs that a man is already attached – he'll either be looking over occasionally at that tall, leggy blonde or she'll come hurtling over, antennae on the alert, at the first sign of any competition.

Nightclubs

Blaring music and dim lighting dictate that clubs are traditionally a meeting place for bodies and not minds. As a result they can be quite daunting, especially if you want to have any kind of conversation on a more meaningful level than 'do you fancy a drink?' Though, having said that, a club is a great place if you want to see what a guy looks like dancing. A girlfriend of mine swears that a cool dancer will be a hot lover – all that being in tune with himself and having good rhythm and so on. Given the constraints on conversation, make sure that if you do meet someone you fancy, either take *their* number and give them a call or just pass on your email address, mobile or work number only. Don't hand out your home phone number to anyone unless you feel sure that you have got to know them just a little bit, and most definitely do not give them your home address for any reason.

Someone who knows someone...

There are times when a friend knows someone who might be 'just perfect' for you or knows someone who knows someone of the same ilk. This can be a quagmire of raised expectations and dashed hopes. He will either be someone just like your last love or the total opposite (and therefore probably deeply unfanciable) or someone who's been single for so long that he's desperate to be fixed up and may be tragically rusty at the dating game as well. But, on the other hand, at least he will have been vetted by someone close to you so it's definitely worth a try... But do try to keep those expectations firmly nailed to the mast, however much your friend tells you this mystery man is fabulous and perfect for you.

Dinner parties

These situations can be a bit like the above and are definitely much more successful if there is a whole mix of people there so you and *he* are not the only singles there. Otherwise, you run the risk that all eyes will be upon you to see how you're reacting to each other and that can be a killer start to any potential new relationship, however gorgeous he is. If you do like him though, use all the tactics mentioned earlier, but dilute them a little so that you can indicate that his further attention would be welcome (but away from prying eyes). Make sure that it's not so obvious that the whole dinner party can see your every move. Try discreetly passing your business card or mobile number to him and then just concentrate on chatting to the rest of the people at the table.

Your workplace

More than half of all long-term couples meet at work. Not surprising really when you take into account just how much time we spend there. You get to see someone as they actually are, without the influence of alcohol or surrounded by their mates, and also how they function under pressure or when dealing with clients or customers. Like what you see? The quickest way from A to Zee is to ask them how their weekend was on a Monday morning. Anyone whose answer begins with a 'We' is probably best not pursued. Alternatively, check out their romantic status with another work colleague, but do make sure that they have your best interests at heart and won't go running straight to him with cries of 'guess who fancies you?' You could always try organizing a group drink after work or try that trusty old ruse 'I've got two tickets to a gig/play/comedy show next week and my flatmate can't come, do you fancy it?' It often works.

Internet dating

There's much more on this in Chapter 13: Love@First Site, and there's a lot to be said for this new world of virtual cyber-dating. There are more than a million of us regularly logging on to internet dating sites and that number is growing all the time. Choose your site with care, though, as some are simply 'meet markets' requiring the most basic of information i.e. age, sex, location. Better sites ask more probing questions about your job, political affiliation (if any), regular newspapers and magazines, level of interest in the arts, sport, travel etc. Go for a reputable site, put up a good picture of yourself, register all your details and for a small sum each month, you can then trawl through hundreds of eligible men on-line.

A word of warning though – not all the men are quite what they seem. Some are married, others older than stated, and many are fatter or balder than their 10-years-out-of-date photo implies. Some are just looking for sex. Some are desperate to get married and have kids. Some simply get off on chatting on-line and disappear when meeting up is suggested or worse still they make an arrangement to meet and then don't turn up. However, there are some decent men out there and experience and gut instinct will help to guide you in the right direction.

Always chat to prospective dates on the phone before meeting up as their manner and voice are important clues as to what sort of person they are and will help you judge whether you like them or not. And of course, always, always, always meet them in a public place where you can make your excuses and leave if you feel in any way uncomfortable. The same applies to meeting people through the personal or 'lonely heart' ads, introduction agencies or any other kind of 'arranged' dating.

The chance meeting

There is always the possibility that you might meet someone somewhere totally unexpected, i.e. in a supermarket (some even hold singles shopping nights these days!), a library, on a train or plane, in a book or record store, at a night class, in an art gallery, whilst out jogging, on holiday or even at the launderette. It's often hard to think of something to say in these circumstances so if in doubt, and you want to seize the moment, a simple 'have you got the time please?' or 'do you know which aisle the cereals are in?' will buy you a bit of time. I actually faked a faint in an art gallery once just so I could get talking to the hunk who was gazing adoringly at a Pre-Raphaelite masterpiece. A little extreme, I know, but it worked brilliantly. He bought me a reviving coffee and we dated successfully for a couple of months, until his love of art eventually took him back to his native Italy. Supermarkets are particularly good as you have the advantage of being able to tell a lot about a man by looking inside his basket! Nappies, baby food and sanitary towels are a bit of a giveaway, as are loaves of sliced white bread, microwave meals for one and frozen oven chips!

Taking time for reflection

Taking a little time out between relationships is never a bad thing as it helps give you time to re-evaluate what you have learned in the past and what you may want out of any new relationship. This may change over time and what you want now may well be quite different from what you will want a year or so down the line.

Beware of stating that you are 'not looking for commitment'. You may not be actively seeking it (especially if you are fresh out of a previous relationship) but advertising it can give *carte blanche* to a man who is simply looking for a little light-hearted fun. It's a phrase that he will never forget and if you get hooked on him six months or so down the line, he'll remind you of your opening gambit time and time again. Be wary of ever playing this card, unless you really do want to remain in an emotional twilight zone and really don't want to become seriously involved with someone. Never say that you are not looking for a committed relationship just because that is what you think he wants to hear. And if you are secretly hoping that his feelings will change, be warned: they rarely do and it's a dangerous game to play with your heart.

When you are dating and deciding what you want out of a new relationship, try to resist the

"Never say you are not looking for a committed relationship just because you think that is what he wants to hear."

temptation to start imagining that you are making some sort of fatal error each time it doesn't work out because you keep picking the 'wrong' guy. This is a crazy concept. While there are some men who are obviously bad and are best avoided (i.e. married, irresponsible or seriously arrogant) you can't really make a decision about a new man until you have dated him a few times. Isn't that what dating is all about? The bad boys (the ones who don't call, mess you about or are control freaks) don't look, smell or sound any different to the good guys who could make you feel great. What you need to do is to take a little time to sort the wheat from the chaff and get to know the men that you date properly before coming to any decision about them. Trust me, most losers will have given themselves away by the third date.

The last – and final – warning is never to assume that the fabulous new man won't hurt you. Even if you have opened your heart, told him about past pain and he has assured you that he would never do that to you and never hurt you, it's important to ask yourself how he can make such rash promises. You may feel absolved, cleansed, protected even, once you've told him all about your broken heart, but you can't dump those feelings on him and expect him not to be true to himself. After all, it wouldn't be much of a relationship if he stayed with you because he promised not to hurt you or because he didn't want to break your heart. Relationships almost always involve hurt at some level and you need to remain aware of this, however blissful it may seem at the beginning. If he can't hurt you then you can only feel indifferent to him. It's just one of those responsibilities to ourselves that we all have to learn.

The Five Golden Rules when starting a new relationship
(Especially important if you've been hurt in the recent past.)

❶ Leave your past behind.
A break-up is often like a bereavement because we go through similar stages of shock, withdrawal, denial, grief and anger. Take support where you can find it – family, friends, colleagues – and keep busy. Go on that diet, build that bookcase or get away for a weekend. But don't take your past with you as you move forward.

❷ Learn the lessons that will help you move forward.
What were the good parts of your last relationship? Could you have been more alert to the danger signs when it started to go wrong? You can't entirely avoid heartache in the future, but you can protect yourself against it to some degree by learning to be more in touch with your feelings and behaviour. When you have learnt to understand yourself better, you can use this emotional honesty in a new relationship.

❸ Get sociable.

Accept as many invitations as you can – from both work colleagues and friends. Call those girlfriends you may have neglected a bit while you were in a relationship. They'll understand as they've been there too. Take up a sport, salsa dancing or join a gym. You'll be more active, increase your chances of meeting new people and feel better about yourself generally.

❹ Learn to recognize the early, basic signs of compatibility.

Is he fun? Is he attractive? Does he have an appealing voice? Do you fancy him? Do you have similar goals and values? Is he really single?

❺ Follow your nose

(not literally, though a man lacking in personal hygiene is not a creature worth pursuing!) and hone your instincts. If it feels right, then it probably is. If you feel uncomfortable or have any nagging doubts about someone, ask questions, take your time and be picky. The more you date, the more finely tuned your instincts will become.

Having fun!

Above all, dating should be fun. It's a chance to meet new people, to have some laughs, to experience that wonderful sense of heightened excitement and, of course, to have great sex. You will no doubt kiss a lot of frogs along the way and spend time with a lot of wolves in sheep's clothing. There may well be men who promise to call but don't, baffling one-night stands, boring men, arrogant men, unfaithful men and so on, but looking for someone fun to date and dating itself, will always enrich your life, even if it doesn't seem that way when it all ends in tears for the umpteenth time. When I was a little girl my mother used to sing me a song: 'Que sera, sera…', which translates as 'Whatever will be, will be…' And that's how I view dating – if it's meant to be, it will happen. Of course you can't just sit back and wait for a date to happen anymore than you can make little or no effort in a relationship and expect it to work out. But if you bring integrity, honesty, dignity, a sense of fun and a little mystery to the table, you will get your just desserts – just as I know that all those cheating, lying and arrogant men will eventually get theirs.

Having established that you want to date and that you're prepared to take the rough with the smooth, it's time to hold your head high and venture forth. Try to be open-minded about what you want from a man. Okay, so you may want your perfect man to have dark floppy hair, great teeth and a body to die for, but your next love might actually turn out to be stocky and blonde but make you laugh and tingle where and when you least expected it. Don't fight it, just go with the flow and try to rid yourself of any preconceived ideas of your ideal. Chemistry is a curious thing and you can find yourself fancying a man who you may previously have considered not to be not your type *because* he makes you laugh and feel adored. To be able to laugh someone into bed is a wonderful thing and remember that plainer men have to try harder – for obvious reasons! I once went out with a fairly overweight guy – definitely not the six pack and bulging pecs that I yearned for and he ended up breaking my heart. I then spent months looking at every hugely over-weight man I saw, thinking he could be the next significant other in my life!

Because dating is meant to be fun, try not to ever – well maybe not until date number three at the earliest – ask yourself the big question: 'Could I spend the rest of my life with this man?' They will most certainly not be ask-ing themselves that question until way further down the line, if ever. Try to think of dating as you would shopping. Buying your perfect wardrobe in one hit would simply take the pleasure out of all those other retail therapy trips. Dating is simply emotional therapy – you'll choose some brilliant pieces that work well in your life for a little while and some supposed bargains that you get tired of after just a few weeks. And occasionally, you'll make a fantastic purchase that becomes a wardrobe/bedroom staple for years to come!

Ten rules to keep dating fun

❶ Live for the moment and not the past or the future.

❷ Be relaxed, charming and keep it light.

❸ Go with the flow and don't over-analyze situations.

❹ Don't dress like a whore or a nun – keep it simple, sexy and sassy.

❺ Don't discuss your date in fine detail with your mates – just give a brief résumé and leave it at that.

❻ If you enjoyed yourself, tell him so.

❼ If you want to see him again – text or call him.

❽ Never feel pressurized into sex on the first date but don't deny yourself if that's what you are sure that you want.

❾ If you don't want to see him again, tell him in a firm but diplomatic way. Don't just avoid his calls. Men have feelings too!

❿ Remember a date is for a few hours, not the rest of your life.

Expectations

It is always worth having realistic expectations, especially if you have recently come out of a relationship and are feeling vulnerable. A lot of 'experts' advise against going straight into another relationship shortly after a break up i.e. 'on the rebound' because it is easy to mistakenly expect the new man to slip conveniently into place and plug the gap left by the previous one. Instead, revel in your rediscovered singledom, take your time to have a little fun and play the field and don't leap into the arms of the first man that appears to offer you stability and comfort. This is not the time for that. This is the time for excitement, a little wildness, no commitment and enormous fun along the way. Men are hugely attracted to independent women who genuinely *want* to be with them, rather than *need* to be with them. If you leave a man wanting, then that's just what he'll do…want you.

The other side of the coin, when you're back on the singles scene again, is that scary creature – the 'Desperate to Date'. We all know these women – they may be stunning with fantastic figures and the wit of Dorothy Parker, but they can't seem to attract and keep a man. There's nothing obviously wrong with these women but it is as if they give off some sort of silent signal to men, alerting them to back off before they've been drawn in and making men unprepared and unwilling to commit.

Actually, contrary to popular opinion, this is not an exclusively female trait. There are many men who, in their unseemly rush to find a life partner, will shower you with questions – all designed to reveal your suitability as a mate. This kind of behaviour from either sex is a definite no-no. It is easy to fall into this trap, especially as you get older – so few men, so little time – but it is majorly off-putting to men, whose initial thoughts are probably more along the lines of 'I wonder what her tits are like' than 'will she make a pretty winter bride?' Maintain your dignity and remain just slightly elusive if you feel that you are in danger of the 'desperate to date' syndrome. Ask questions only because you genuinely want to find out more about someone else not because you're wondering what they look like in a tux or whether their earning capacity can keep you in designer labels for the rest of your days. Remember men love a woman who is warm, funny, honest and just slightly out of their reach.

"Remain just slightly elusive if you feel that you are in danger of the 'desperate to date' syndrome."

Another danger point when starting over is to make the mistake of not giving enough of yourself and being too suspicious and cynical of any new mate, because of the way you've been treated in the past. I have seen many potentially good relationships founder because a previously disappointed woman was cynical and wouldn't give her new relationship a fighting chance. Bitterness can often manifest itself as sarcasm and while a sharp, dry wit can be enormously attractive to men, cutting cynicism is rarely so. You can be a little guarded and discreetly look out for any danger signs, whilst still being warm, fun and flirtatious.

Another definite no-no when you are embarking on a new relationship is discussing your previous one. Your bitterness and resentment, or simply your longing and sadness, will have most men running for the hills however kind-hearted and sympathetic he seems to be at the time. It will always appear to him that you are comparing him with other men and not giving him a chance to shine for himself. While men relish the thrill of the chase, they like – at least at first – to have your undivided attention and a blank canvass upon which to impress you. It is natural for you to exchange this sort of information as your relationship progresses – it is an essential part of getting to know each other – but on the first few dates it is better to either touch upon old relationships *en passant* and minus the gory details, or not at all!

Sex

So, we've reached the stage where you're willing, ready and able to give the dating game another go. Great. That brings us, of course, to sex and the question: 'When is the time right in a new relationship?' My personal view would be after date two, three or four – when the excitement is still raw and the *frisson* is starting to build. If the chemistry's definitely there, he makes you laugh, the only appetite you've really got is a sexual one and you're start-ing to like and trust this guy, it's probably a sign that the time is right. But, it is entirely an individual choice. If you feel ready and comfortable on the first date, go for it. If you want to wait a month or more, then wait, just do what feels right. But I do want to sound two warnings from the bows here... Wait too long, and that gorgeous, attractive, seemingly patient man just might wander into an adjacent field where the grass is greener and definitely fresh-er! When a man is not sleeping with a woman, he can often think that he's not really in a relationship at all. Curiously, if you do the opposite and willingly jump into bed on the first date he might think you're too easy when he, of course, is just doing what comes naturally and what's expected of him. While some men totally accept that a woman sleeping with them on the first night is fine and proper and implies nothing but a healthy level of lust (if you find this rare creature hang onto him!) most wrestle with a constant dilemma. They'll wine and dine you, schmooze, flirt and do anything to get your knick-ers off on the first date, but while a huge part of their minds is urging you to say 'yes', another part is wanting you to say 'no' to show them that you are not simply an easy lay, or worse still, a slapper, slag or whatever other choice words some men have for a woman who is also just doing what comes naturally. Definitely do not sleep with someone on the first date when you've had too much to drink. Guilt, regret and nausea are not what you should be feeling the following morning!

I have known men who in spite of their initial, keen impressions of a woman, sleep with her on the first date, have great sex and then don't bother to call again and so she becomes that miserable thing – the 'one-night stand'. Even in the 21st century, this is still predominantly a male domain, whether they began the night with that thought in mind or not. I certainly don't know too many women who go out with the intention of getting pissed, pulling and post-coitally dumping. You can never completely avoid what one friend of mine quaintly calls the "fuck 'em and chuck 'em merchants" but you stand less chance of being a victim if you keep them on their toes for a date or two longer. It's also not nearly as common to jump into bed on the first date as many of us seem to think. The Durex Global Sex Survey in 2002 found that only 17 per cent of people expect to go the whole way on the first night and only 24 per cent within the first month of a new relationship. So don't feel pressurized, don't feel abnormal and do what feels right for you at the time. Even if you're older, very experienced and definitely no virgin, there are still times when sex feels okay and times when it doesn't. Never base your decision simply on your hopes for the future of a new relationship or on your fear of jeopardizing it early on.

Chapter 2
the single life
alone versus lonely

First, let's establish what we mean by being alone and what we mean by being lonely. Alone is a descriptive state. I'm typing this book alone. No one else is in the house, it's a Sunday afternoon, I'm listening to some Latin American music on my CD player and I've got a glass of chilled Chablis at my side. Am I lonely? Most definitely not! I'm actually quite happy about being alone right now. I have space, independence, no make-up on and I'm at peace with myself. Greta Garbo once famously said 'I vant to be alone' and we all need that solitude from time to time in order to gather our thoughts, eat toast and Marmite in bed with the Sunday papers, catch up on paperwork or simply watch our favourite soap in peace. It can be a pretty good state of affairs all in all, as long as it doesn't take over our lives.

Even then, a protracted period of 'aloneness' isn't the same as being lonely. Loneliness is a state of mind, reflecting the individual's mood. It has nothing to do with physical proximity to other people but everything to do with intimacy, the life blood of what makes us function as contented and fulfilled people. You can be lonely when you're busy, when you're half of a couple and even when you're in a crowded room.

When a relationship comes to an end you often find yourself spending much more time alone. With that, comes a significant sense of loss – loss of love, companionship, and daily routine. If you are able to reflect on the past and have the determination to move on you will find solace in solitude and a feeling of space and freedom. If you hide away and mourn, the sense of loneliness merely intensifies. The quiet around you accentuates your loss and feelings of restlessness and a lack of motivation makes even watching TV, reading or doing simple household tasks seem pointless.

Pigeon Steps

Try to think of being alone as challenging – a release from your routine that opens up all sorts of possibilities previously denied you. Taking pigeon steps to sorting this out is critical – a giant leap into a new life, filling every waking hour with friends, social activities and work will go some way towards healing the pain, but you'll exhaust yourself and be unable to cope with the bad days that can take you by surprise at any time. So you need to take steps to change your lifestyle, in order for you to feel better about being alone. Find a few activities that you know you enjoy or that may have been difficult for you to do as part of a couple. Join a gym, take up jogging or painting – or whatever makes you feel good. Try a few things out for size and see what fits you best. Take up again with those neglected friends. Simply making arrangements helps to break the cycle of inertia and listlessness that sets in when loneliness takes over.

"Take up one or two new activities or return to some that may have been difficult for you to keep up as part of a couple. Why not join a gym, take up jogging or learn to paint?"

Learn to feel comfortable being alone. One of my greatest pleasures after the break up of a major relationship is to go out and buy a whole heap of CDs (the kind of music that my partner didn't particularly care for) and play them over and over again. I also watch a lot of TV and listen to the radio constantly. I've found that having a voice or two in the background gives me some comfort and reminds me that I'm not totally alone in the world. I also find that I start working harder – initially in order to make the day go faster – but then, for the first time in ages, I actually start to feel that I am getting somewhere and that I'm on top of my workload. All these things eventually start to add up and begin to create a renewed sense of fulfilment and well-being.

Fear of being lonely

One of the biggest trends in the 21st century is to be constantly busy. We overload our lives and always feel under pressure to be doing something or seeing someone. Who's alone on a Saturday night, we ask ourselves? Or on a Thursday, Friday or Sunday night? Or a Sunday lunchtime? We relentlessly plan and fill our days to avoid emptiness and feel that's there's always something to look forward to.

My friend Lucy has such a packed diary that I have to book weeks ahead to see her and even then it's often just a quick, early evening drink before she dashes off to yet another dinner party or a Pilates class. It used to make me think that she was the most popular person on earth and by contrast I was Ms Billy-no-mates. Then it occurred to me that she was shielding herself from loneliness and was addicted to going out and meeting people to avoid that terrible fear of being alone and not knowing how to cope. As well as draining her bank account and giving herself stratospheric mobile phone bills she then came seriously unstuck when she met a guy she actually wanted to date. The only 'window' she had was three weeks away on a Wednesday night between 5.30pm and 7.00pm! She finally relented, cancelled an arrangement or two and made the effort. Even though the relationship was relatively short lived, she came to understand that there was no real need to live every waking moment in a constant social whirl.

By actually deciding to be alone for a while you are making a brave and independent choice. And you might be surprised when you find that by spending time alone, feelings of loneliness, as well as the fear of that loneliness, will dissipate in a way that you might not have imagined possible. Fear of any kind – whether it's of spiders, the dark or flying – is debilitating because we allow it to hold us back and stop us from doing certain things. But fear of loneliness is a double whammy, because the very act of withdrawing from the thing we fear creates the exact thing that we are afraid of! Being lonely. And if this sounds like psychobabble, believe me, it isn't – read it again, it makes sense!

Learning to enjoy your own company

Some people seem to love their own company and relish every opportunity to spend time alone. Most of us need to learn to love ourselves before we feel truly comfortable on our own. It's one of the greatest skills that you can learn, because not only does it keep loneliness at bay, it also makes you a more interesting person to spend time with.

"Take pleasure in exercising the right to enjoy your freedom in the way that you want to."

While the tale of my friend Lucy (above) is a salutary one, it does pay to plan ahead to some degree. Consider all those things that you never really have time to do and create a little 'me' time. Keep it to one night a week at first. It might be something simple like a regular manicure and pedicure or a long hot soak in a candle-lit bath full of essential oils. Or perhaps it's something more ambitious, like learning to rockclimb or taking a diving course at your local swimming pool.

Whatever you choose to do, make sure that you indulge yourself fully. Make that bath really special – buy the best oils, bubbles and potions that you can afford, surround yourself with candles, play your favourite CD, take the phone off the hook and switch off your mobile. Make sure your sheets are crisp and clean and savour the moment when you slide into them.

During a prolonged single period of my life, I used to pay an exorbitant sum to have my sheets laundered once a week so that I could hear the linen crackle as I got into bed after my sensuous bath. Trust me, it can feel as good as any orgasm. Take pleasure in exercising the right to enjoy your freedom in the way that you want to. It's unique, you've tailored it to your own specifications and any sense of exhilaration and achievement is all yours. After all, there are no compromises and there's no one to please but yourself.

> **"The more 'me' time you indulge in, the more you will learn to love yourself - and the more love you will have to give to a future partner."**

One of the key lessons here is not only to learn to love yourself and be happy in your own company, but also to lose the dependency of 'needing' a relationship and feeling incomplete when you are not part of a couple. How often do we still hear that awful phrase, 'my other half'? However good intimacy makes us feel – there's no denying that the adrenaline rush is a fantastic feeling – it is emotionally unhealthy to depend on a relationship to sustain those feelings or to feel unworthy or miserable without one. We've all known people who seem to stick with a less than satisfying relationship because they feel too insecure to be on their own or are scared of the supposed stigma of being single again.

So, to summarize, take as much 'me' time as you can. Work on developing yourself as an individual. By all means look at your weaknesses, maybe even try and work on them, but remember that this is the time to take a positive attitude to life and form a good relationship with yourself. After all it is the one relationship that's going to see you through the good times and the bad, until the bitter end… Be proud of your achievements, be brave, be bold and just see how brilliantly the confident and relaxed new you performs in a relationship when it comes along. One of the biggest rewards is discovering that the more 'me' time you indulge in, the more you learn to love yourself and the more love you will have to give to a future partner.

The good things about being single

As well as all the above, there are loads of other benefits of being single, especially if you don't let yourself see it as a permanent state of affairs but a valuable pause in the dating game. As well as being able to choose what *you* eat for supper – and indeed whether you want any supper at all or want to eat it with your fingers at midnight! – you can also choose how you spend your money, how to decorate your home and where you go on holiday. You are answerable to no one but yourself. It's all take and no give and while this lack of compromise may seem alien at first, you'll soon get a taste for it. I enjoy my space so much these days that I can't imagine living with someone again 24/7, however much I might yearn for the intimacy, companionship and sex of a good relationship at times!

Freedom can open up all sorts of possibilities. You can shop until you drop and you can watch that slushy movie (and sob with abandon) on a Saturday afternoon when *he* used to be watching the footie results. You can read a book in one sitting without fear of interruption, wear that oh-so-comfy – but deeply unsexy – nightdress and fluffy slippers combo. The list is endless. And if you've never gone to the cinema on your own – try it. See all those friends of yours that he was never that keen on – or they on him. Develop a platonic friendship with that nice guy at work and have a few drinks with him to get the male perspective for a change. There's no risk of the boyfriend getting jealous or arsey now, is there?

You could even completely reinvent yourself. Maybe this would be a good opportunity for you to change your career? Or maybe you've always wanted to travel or wanted to live abroad for a year or so? Now that you have no one but yourself to please, you can be spontaneous without worry or guilt. You can enjoy flirting with younger men, waiters and barmen and have fun on endless girlie nights out with your friends with no anxieties.

Don't make love – have sex!

While there's much to be said for great love-making within the confines of an intimate, loving relationship, there's also an amazing time to be had out there having wild sex, having a quick shag or whatever else takes your fancy. Provided you're not hurting anyone else – or yourself, of course – and you've got a plentiful supply of condoms, you can now make a play for that oh-so sexy but not so bright guy at the gym or that cute but far-too-young barman at your local.

If you've never tried non-committal sex, you'll be amazed at how liberating and enjoyable it can be. Once you've dumped any emotional baggage you can completely indulge in the sheer physicality of it all. You can play with the most unlikely of men, hone your sexual skills, explain exactly what you want and experiment with him to your heart's content. You can put on the performance of a lifetime and take the applause or you can just lie back and enjoy it. Who cares if your partner might not be marriage material or that your friends and family would deem him totally unsuitable? You are enjoying fantastic, unadulterated, totally hedonistic sex. Go girl!

"If you've never tried non-committal sex, you'll be amazed at how liberating and enjoyable it can be."

Fifteen reasons to celebrate singledom

The list of reasons to enjoy singledom is endless but in case you remain unconvinced, here (in no particular order) are my personal favourites. Why not write your own list to remind yourself what you enjoy about life, being single and being free from constraints? Whether they're things you couldn't do because of a relationship or just dropped, revisit them and learn to enjoy life as a single person again.

❶ I no longer have to wash his smelly socks and dubious underwear.

❷ I can have another drink/cigarette/bar of chocolate and no one's going to complain or make 'tsk-tsk' noises at me.

❸ I can take ownership of my orgasms and not have to fake one or make flimsy excuses if I don't fancy sex.

❹ I can lie diagonally across a double bed and wriggle about all I want.

❺ I can watch TV in bed at 3.00am without fear of disturbing or irritating anyone else.

❻ I no longer have to be kept awake by his snoring.

❼ I can be extravagant and spend a small fortune on shoes without having to lie about the cost or pretend that I've had them for ages.

❽ I can eat what I want, when I want and how I want.

❾ I can use both sides of my wardrobe.

❿ I can buy a great bottle of white wine and drink it all myself.

⓫ I can spend all evening on the phone to my closest girl friends without him nagging that I 'only saw her yesterday'.

⓬ I don't have to remember his mother's/sister's/nephew's birthdays for him.

⓭ I can go to the loo and leave the door open.

⓮ I can listen to my music whenever I want to.

⓯ I can practise salsa dancing and do workouts in front of the TV with no one to criticize my wobbly bits (why on earth did he think that I was exercising in the first place!!?).

Enjoy your singledom while you can

There are around 12 million unmarried people in the UK and over four million singles aged between 25 and 44 so you've got plenty of company. Always remember that you can nearly always go out and meet or pull someone if you really want to and that being single can be empowering not debilitating. There is absolutely no social stigma attached to being single.

As a singleton, you are likely to live longer, suffer less stress, be better off financially and a good deal more independent. In fact there are so many reasons to celebrate and relish the single lifestyle that I firmly believe more and more people will be embracing it through choice in the coming years, rather than having it thrust upon them. As a singleton, instead of relying on one person for all your emotional and practical support you are forced to widen the net and develop a broader and more varied social network, which means you can indulge in a whole range of activities and experience more of what life has to offer.

Your biological clock can tick louder and longer – it's probably not until our mid- to late-thirties that we really need to make a decision about starting a family. Less responsibility means lower stress levels, which in turn means higher libidos and more freedom to exploit them. And perhaps the best news of all – given that this book is all about dating – is that if you are content and comfortable being single your chances of meeting the right guy will increase significantly!

Chapter 3
Expectations
knowing what you want

While it's dangerous to go in search of 'The Perfect Man' when seeking a date, it's always wise to have a few minimum expectations at the outset, otherwise you've got no parameters to work within. And by expectations, I really mean a sort of wish list of the kind of qualities that you'd ideally like your man to have. Your wish list is bound to include a few physical factors – slim build, nice eyes, tall etc. but try not to make these too precise or you'll miss out on dating opportunities because men simply don't fit your criteria. Going for a 6-foot tall, blue-eyed Adonis with dark floppy-hair will certainly focus the search, but it might just narrow the field too much.

A shared sense of humour is always an important factor. That perennial GSOH so beloved of the small ads is a tad woolly – after all, who's going to say that they've got a BSOH, even if they only laugh at Tom and Jerry cartoons and Jim Davidson! What is your sense of humour? Dry, witty and sophisticated or laugh out loud? I was once mortified to read in an article that I 'giggled'. I don't giggle! In fact I rarely laugh out loud. But when I do find someone who tickles my unique sense of humour then I'll laugh until I cry. But giggle? Not me – never. I love to tease, but I don't enjoy being teased myself. I can be surprisingly naïve and gullible at times and being teased makes me feel uncomfortable. Some people love to be teased though. Think about your own humour style.

The sound of someone's voice is another big factor for me. I'm not great with squeaky, camp voices (in spite of the fact that some of my best friends are gay). I also dislike the 'ok-yah' posh accent and that dreadful mockney, 'fort I'd adopt a bitta street cred' voice, although I love the genuine article. But I love a Geordie accent. And a soft Southern Irish lilt. And a French accent. And especially a deep, velvety, sexy voice. Remember, you're going to hear his voice a lot – phone calls, sweet nothings and maybe even the 'lurve' declaration, so make sure that it's one that you can live with. It is also worth remembering that while endearing traits such as a loveable but crooked smile can become even more endearing as time passes, irritating mannerisms such as using odd or bizarre phrases repeatedly or having a silly laugh, rarely do. They simply get more and more irritating, sometimes even becoming one of the main reasons for ending the relationship!

Whatever your expectations may be, and however little you are willing to compromise, be open-minded and prepared to let that wide world of dating experience refine and broaden them over time. And although you are constantly bombarded by the most delicious, sexy, cute guys looking out at you from every movie screen, advertising billboard and magazine page, try to stay realistic. If you don't 'keep it real' you might find that your overly-high expectations will yield few results.

The Perfect Man

HE DOESN'T EXIST. And if he did and he was mine, I'd live in a permanent state of frayed nerves, constantly worried that the moment he stepped out of the front door it would be straight into the arms of a shinier-haired, leggier, bigger-breasted and slimmer girl than me. I would have to keep him under lock and key and bring him out for special occasions only, preferably under cover of darkness and preferably into male-only gatherings. What does exist, however, is the guy who is perfect for you now and who has more than a hint of the sort of someone you could grow old with. You will not know him at first sight. Sorry to be so negative but love at first sight just ain't possible. Longing, lust, desire – they're all possible at first sight. But love – never! It is possible to know that you could have the capacity to love someone after a date or two, but it can't flourish into anything lasting for some time after that. Dating is a double-edged sword and lurking behind that gorgeous façade could be a mean-spirited person. While getting to know someone, you will experience both the good and the bad. He may be all that you wanted in a man, but the more you see of him, the more time you spend getting to know each other, he will invariably reveal certain traits, personal habits and behaviour

EVERY GIRL'S GUIDE TO FINDING THE PERFECT MAN

1 It is important to find a man who works around the house, occasionally cooks and cleans and who has a good job.

2 It is important to find a man who makes you laugh.

3 It is important to find a man who is dependable and doesn't lie.

4 It is important to find a man who's good in bed and who loves to have sex with you.

5 It is very important that these four men never meet...

that you may grow to love, but wouldn't be on your initial wish list. And that's just how it should be.

If you're too much in love with the idea of finding 'The Perfect Man', then you're just too picky. For example, I knew a girl who was obsessed by men's feet. They are rarely objects of beauty, but as well as hating all the usual stuff like grubby trainers, white socks and socks with sandals, she became obsessed with what lay below. Yellowing toenails and dry skin are always ugly, but she hated hair on feet, high insteps and bony toes! And unless she pulled on the beach or at a swimming pool, she had to go way past first base to discover just what her new man's feet were like! There were a million other things she didn't 'do' either. Receding hairlines, holding a wine glass by the stem, trouser belts (!), less than perfect buttocks, tattoos, jewellery, opera, rugby, less than perfect teeth, wiry hair, smoking, V-necked jumpers, laughing like Mutley, working out less than three times a week and so on. I have to say that she's gorgeous-looking with a real sense of fun (lest you think she's a complete control freak!) and amazingly she did manage more than her fair share of dates, but by date three nearly all of her conquests had – not surprisingly – failed on at least three counts. Keeping certain standards is critical to self-esteem, but going too far in your search for perfection will leave you disappointed and dateless. Especially when you consider the average man's simplistic idea of a perfect woman. Shut your eyes and guess what I'm going to say, before you read it… Yup, you've got it – tall, blonde and busty.

It's all down to our expectations. Get a little less demanding, inject a little compromise into your wannabe list and you'll get a hell of a lot more fun along the way. Focus on a few of the really critical dating variables and make an effort to overlook the others. Even if he doesn't look like George Clooney but he makes you laugh, let him laugh your knickers off. Keep refining that list and avoid becoming a snob or a gold digger. The wider the variety of people you date, the greater the chance you have of meeting someone who is right for you.

Projection

Projection is like wearing a blindfold. It can happen when you catch the eye of a man and in an instant project upon him what you want him to be. You look beyond the fact that he's actually not tall and slim but short and rather stout. You want him to be in his mid-twenties, so that's what you imagine him to be. Actually, he's nearer forty. Is he well-dressed or trendy? Nope, he's scruffy and crumpled, but he seems to be able to get away with it. There's nothing inherently wrong in projection – in fact it can make you re-evaluate what may be overly demanding criteria – but it is something you should be aware that you are doing. I once met a lovely guy on a long train journey. Being in my mid-thirties, I imagined him to be in his early thirties. Perfect. He told me he was doing a degree in IT. I commented that I thought it was brave to go back and do a course or take a change of direction when you were older. He looked at me quizzically. Yup, he turned out to be 22! When I looked a little closer, I realized that I had been an idiot. I didn't want to develop a relationship with a man of 22, and so by wanting him to be my ideal age, he became so in my eyes. He, I suspect, knew exactly how old I was, but was attracted by the cache of sexual experience, wisdom and freedom that men love to think that older women all have!

Projection only becomes a cause for concern when your desire for this man to be what you want him to be is so strong that you go into a state of emotional denial. You have a sneaking suspicion that he's not exactly what you originally saw, but you hope that he'll change. Or worse still you try and change him. It is worth remembering that men can be relatively uncomplicated creatures. The reason that he's not resisting your attempt to change him isn't because he's happy to go along with it, but simply because he hasn't actually realized what's going on! When the penny drops, he's more than likely to take cover or cut and run. Trust me.

Making your wish list

Sometimes it helps to write down your wish list. Divide it into 'must-haves' e.g. 'is solvent', 'lives in same town as me' etc and 'would like if possible but accept it might just be a bonus', such as 'has dark, floppy hair' (a recurrent theme, I know, no prizes for guessing why…) or 'having a similar career as me'. Here are some of the factors that you might want to consider when compiling your list:

❶ Do you want him to be your best friend as well as your partner?

❷ Are you looking for long-term commitment or something else?

❸ Do you want to be able to laugh at the same things as him?

❹ If you are looking for commitment and want a family one day, could you imagine having his babies?

❺ What level of independence do you want to retain i.e. are you looking for 24/7 togetherness?

❻ Is it important to you that your libidos match?

❼ Could you cope with, or do you actively want, a relationship where monogamy is not an issue?

8 Do you expect complete devotion or would a jealous man send you heading for the hills?

9 Do you admire ruthless ambition and drive in a man or would someone who just goes with the flow suit you better?

10 Do you feel you need someone on your intellectual or cultural level?

11 Do you want someone near your own age or would an older or younger man appeal to you?

12 Is instant physical chemistry critical or do you believe that it can develop in time?

13 Do you mind/want a smoker? A drinker? Or a gym junkie?

Be realistic about yourself

Tough though it can be, it's an invaluable exercise to stand back and take an honest look at yourself. How desirable are you? How attractive? What kind of man is likely to go for a girl like you? It's worth drafting in a close friend to help with this. Someone who you respect and whose opinion you really value. A male friend would be particularly good, especially if you're in the fortunate but rare position of still being mates with an ex. A word of caution though, if either of you is secretly hoping to woo the other back, this exercise will not work! You need to ask them a series of questions and you'll need to be prepared for answers you might not expect or like. (I was mortified once to find that a male chum thought that my leather-clad rock chick look was more like mutton dressed as lamb!) Try these for size:

How attractive are you?

Do you think I'm attractive to men?

How would you rate my attractiveness on a scale of one to ten?

What could I do to improve my rating?

Do you think I'm sexy?

How would you rate my sexiness on a scale of one to ten?

What could I do to become sexier?

Am I a fun person to be with?

Do I seem outgoing or shy to you?

Do I dress well?

Do my clothes suit me?

Am I bright, well-read and interesting?

Do I flirt with men?

Do I flirt too much or too little?

When I'm talking to men do I seem too interested or too aloof?

Do I seem relaxed when I meet a guy or am I a little scary?

Am I too full-on or too passive?

You get the drift… It will not always be a pleasant experience, but you might find that it helps to see things from a different perspective. If the responses are exactly what you expected, then try someone else, because they're probably just saying what they think you want to hear. This is meant to be a 'cruel to be kind' exercise, not a mutual back-scratching – or back-stabbing – event. However, if the answers are too harsh, it's probably time to change your mates! Answer the following questions honestly – it will help you see what you have to offer a potential partner:

❶ Are you good company and interesting to be with?
How are your conversational skills? Do you read a daily paper and watch the news? Or is the limit of your conversation restricted to the soaps? Are you passionate about a hobby or your work? Can you convey this without being boring or dull? Do you ask questions because you have genuine interest in someone else or simply because you want to size them up?

❷ Are you responsive to others?
Do you listen well and give people a chance to say their bit or do you interrupt and butt in all the time with your views?

❸ Are you financially secure?
You don't have to be rich or flash with your cash, but managing your money wisely gives you confidence and allows you to see your date as a person rather than a meal ticket. Dating a wealthy man is great, but see it

as a bonus rather than a goal. If a man thinks you are after him for his money, he will be guarded from the start.

❹ Are you independent?

Do you have goals and aspirations that are your own and not dependent on someone else? Goals that are not just about finding a guy to be with, but goals for yourself, like learning a foreign language, becoming your own boss or running the marathon. These goals are not the same thing as having hobbies – these are major aspirations that you want to work and aim for to boost your own personal self-esteem. It demonstrates that you have ambition and drive as well as independence and is often not only very attractive to men but also very fulfilling for you as a person.

❺ Do you live for the present?

While looking to the future and making plans is an essential part of life, daydreamers who always think that the grass is greener on the other side

DUMPED! HOW TO SPOT THE SIGNS

Sometime, somewhere along the line you're going to get dumped and occasionally just when you least expect it. It happens to all of us, and there's little you can do to legislate against the pain, hurt, surprise, anger and indignity of it all.

However, you can learn to recognize signs of imminent danger. One of these signs on their own isn't necessarily anything to panic about – they are quite often just symptomatic of a little selfishness or a lack of consideration – but if they happen with increasing frequency or in pairs (or higher multiples!) then you need to start taking stock, arming yourself against rejection, or better still, get in there first and dump him before he can get to you!

'Sorry babe, but no time to see you this week.'

Not necessarily a sign of imminent dumping or rejection in itself, especially if you know your man has a work project to finish or is under pressure, but if it comes out of the blue or involves a cancelled date it could indicate a cooling in the relationship or even that he is playing away (or at least thinking about it). Generally we all have roughly the same amount of leisure time each week, give or take family commitments or unusual working hours. You'll soon get to recognize the pattern of his leisure time and where you fit into it. A sudden change in this should certainly make your antennae twitch do not make for good company. Enjoying today and taking life one step at a time can make you a much more relaxed person. It's liberating to free yourself from thoughts of what might lie ahead. Just think how good you feel when you're on holiday! It's even worse if you dwell too much on your emotional past. It can make you cynical, mistrustful and allows anyone who hurt you in the past to carry right on hurting you in the present. Put it behind you. It's time to move on.

❻ Are you a positive person?

Are you happy with your self-image? Are you an optimist or a pessimist? Do you whinge and whine or tackle your problems head on, one at a time? Happiness and healthy self-esteem are infectious and make people want to become part of your life. Negative people create just the opposite effect. Work out what makes you happy and go for it. Accept compliments with good grace and a smile, not suspicion. Learn to recognize your strengths and work on your weaknesses and be the best person you can be.

if nothing else. Most of us feel we are too busy – it's symptomatic of 21st century life – but if we really want something we somehow manage to find time for it, don't we? Suddenly finding that your guy doesn't have as much time as usual, could mean that he doesn't have as much interest in, or enthusiasm for, the relationship as before.

'You can be one scary woman honey, but I love it'

No he doesn't. He might want to love it but actually your confidence, ambition and drive is starting to threaten his alpha male status and it's jostling uncomfortably with his own position in the relationship. He may have loved it at first, but now it's becoming a little more difficult to handle. It's great when you take control in the bedroom or don those thigh-high boots and whip, but not so great if you're going to be more successful than him at work. I know this to my cost. One of my ex boyfriends was really encouraging when I wanted to shoot for the moon jobwise, but when I got the job and thrived on it and started to feel really good about myself, he became increasingly resentful and jealous. Even in this modern world, it's sometimes difficult for men to shake off the ancient Stone Age right to be the chief breadwinner and the head honcho in a relationship. They may become arrogant or possessive or just distance themselves, but once they see this situation as a threat, I'm afraid that they're as good as gone, however much reassurance you might give them.

'I'm so glad you've become such a good friend to me'

Uh-oh. It sounds great doesn't it? And it can be great provided that you're still having just as much sex as before and it's still good. If your sex life has dwindled for any reason, this phrase is seriously scary. Men don't need friends like women do. They need their mum, their sister, a drinking/football/badminton partner and someone to lean on when things aren't going their way. If you become a mixture of these things and your sex life is not as exciting as it once was, then it's a danger sign. Sure, you've got to be friends to make any relationship work long-term, but if you notice your sex life is starting to lack excitement or regularity, then he may just be feeling a little restless. Take it up a notch, don't let him walk through the door and tell you all about his day – go out for dinner, seduce him, arrange to do something out of the ordinary and keep the spark alight .

'I'd love to go out this week but I haven't got any money'

Or 'I have got money, but I can think of better things to spend it on than you'... Money's a bit like time, there's usually a little bit to spare. And if not, a walk in the park or coming over to your flat to watch a movie on the TV costs nothing. It's about value. Does he still value you enough to spend £20 on a meal out or would he prefer to spend it on football this weekend or going to the pub with the boys? Watch out for this one – it's often symptomatic of waning interest.

'Sorry I haven't had a chance to return your call/text/email darling, it's been one of those weeks'

Yeah right. Sure it has. Who *has* he managed to call/text/email then? Don't sit about waiting to hear from him, especially in an established relationship. I love the facility on my mobile that let's me know when a text has been delivered. An ex told me that he was going to the US for two weeks and that his phone wouldn't work out there. So, how come a text I sent him was delivered and received within moments? And how come he then answered his home phone when I called up? I know it might seem a little sinister, but I already had my suspicions and it was a convenient way of checking up on him and I really enjoyed telling him he was dumped over the phone, before he could butt in with any excuses! No decent boyfriend is *ever* too busy to call, mail or send a brief text. And if he is, he isn't interested any more or he is beginning to take you for granted.

Chapter 4

Self-confidence
and
self-esteem

learning to love yourself

Mirror, mirror...

These two expressions are frequently lumped together and while I don't want to bore you to death with the formal psychological definitions of the two – and, anyway, for the purposes of this book you can think of them as virtually interchangeable – there are significant differences between them that it is worth understanding more about.

Confidence is undoubtedly an important element of self-esteem, and people who have a high level of self-esteem (i.e. feel good about themselves, especially in regard to other people) generally have a similar level of confidence in their approach to everyday life. However, there are a number of seemingly confident people, who, once that veneer is scratched away, actually have very poor self-esteem – that is, they are not really comfortable or happy in themselves. In these cases, over-confidence is actually a sign that someone is compensating for a lack of self-esteem, and that's often when we encounter overbearing and arrogant people. Essentially they are covering up for their lack of self-esteem with false confidence and while some people are wise enough to recognize this about themselves, many are not. They adopt a persona that may make them the life and soul of the party, but they often lack many close or loyal friends as a result.

Once you're armed with this information, you will find it relatively easy to spot those smart-arse guys out there who suffer from a serious lack of self-esteem and over-compensate by adopting that 'come and get me! How can you resist this?' approach. Be warned though, if this is the type of man that appeals to you, bear in mind that you will need to get to know him very well before he will feel comfortable enough to be able to make any changes to his outward behaviour. What this means is that both you and your friends and family will have to deal with him until then.

Unfortunately, having a healthy level of self-esteem is not something we are born with. It is something that develops over time and is intrinsically linked to our family, education, work and relationship history. It is also not a 'fixed asset'. It can fluctuate over the years, depending on how life is treating us at any given time. However, just as some individuals are naturally extrovert or introvert, optimistic or pessimistic, most people have a general predisposition to having either a more positive or a more negative attitude towards themselves. Believing in yourself and knowing that you matter will help you to create an environment in which your self-esteem can grow and thrive.

"Overbearing and arrogant people are covering up for their lack of self-esteem with false confidence."

Improving your own level of self-esteem

If you can answer 'yes' to at least ten of the following questions, then you probably have reasonably good self-esteem. Any less than seven positive answers and it's time to take a long look at what is holding you back in learning to be happy in yourself.

Try to be honest and don't answer 'yes' simply because that's how you'd *like* to feel, rather than how you *actually* feel.

❶ Do you like yourself as a person?

❷ Do you think that you deserve to be loved?

❸ Have you something worth giving to someone else (emotionally that is)?

❹ Are you basically a decent, caring person?

❺ Do you deserve to be happy?

❻ Are you generally optimistic about your life?

❼ Do you feel that your opinions matter even if they seem to be different from other people's?

❽ When you do well are you proud of your achievements?

❾ Can you express yourself in company with ease?

❿ Do you find it relatively easy to say 'no'?

⓫ Do you tackle problems individually rather than let them stack up?

⓬ Can you take constructive criticism?

⓭ Do you manage to control your anger or temper?

⓮ Do you find it easy to make good friends?

⓯ Do you willingly take risks, knowing that making mistakes is an essential part of moving forward?

Giving yourself time and space

People with low self-esteem are often constantly busy – they arrange their lives that way. They need to be doing something or seeing people on an almost constant basis because essentially they don't feel happy or relaxed in their own company. If you recognize elements of your own life in this description, take a little time out to be on your own. Stay in for the night, take the phone off the hook and switch off the TV, put your feet up and just relax. Learning the basic principles of meditation can be helpful here. Make yourself do it for half an hour at least three times a week. It may feel strange at first, but after a few weeks, you will learn to love that time and space you've given yourself and will have learnt, most importantly, that you deserve it.

The power of positive thinking

However low your self-esteem may be, there will certainly be things about yourself that you feel are 'not too bad'. Some of these could be physical qualities: nice hair, good skin or slim ankles. Focus on these things and appreciate them. People with higher self-esteem are not necessarily born slimmer or more attractive than those with a lower level of self-esteem but they spend a little time on themselves to work on their appearance and bring out the best in themselves. It is no coincidence that when life throws crap at you i.e. the end of a relationship, the loss of a job etc., most people tend to let themselves go and, inevitably, they experience a loss of self-esteem. While this is an important rite of passage and necessary in order to get over life's difficulties, there also comes a time when – as the song says – you've just got to 'get yourself up, dust yourself down and start all over again!'

Although it's often harder to work on non-physical characteristics than on your appearance, try to accentuate the positive nonetheless, rather than dwelling on the negative, and make improvements to aspects of your life that you are not so happy about. Rather than dwell on all the bad parts of a past relationship, for example, try to remember the good times. If you've had yet another bad day at work, it may well be time to think about changing jobs. However, it may be that your negative attitude means that you are only recalling the bad bits about your day and that if you take a little time to think about it, there were some good bits too! What were they? Write them down if it helps, so that you can take a look at the list another time and remind yourself to adopt a more positive attitude every day.

Also remind yourself of other important factors that contribute towards self-esteem that can easily be overlooked. Are you a generous person? Loyal? Caring? Reliable? Witty? A good listener? Each one of us has something to offer that can be enjoyed and appreciated by someone else. Learning to recognize this is a major step towards improving your self-esteem. Remember, if you value yourself, it makes it much easier for others to value you too.

Natural self-confidence

Self-confident people seem to have all the fun. Throw them into any social situation, however new or bizarre, and they pop up smiling, witty, ready with the right words at the right time. Don't you just hate 'em?! Do you wonder what they've got that you haven't and where you can go to get some of that stuff? You might find it reassuring to know that that even supremely self-confident people are not confident all of the time. Just like shyness, it can fluctuate depending on the circumstances. Being dumped, losing your job or just having situations back-firing unexpectedly can be real killers even for confident people. The point to remember is that these things happen to everyone from time to time, the only difference is that confident people recover from setbacks much faster.

It's all too easy to compare yourself unfavourably to that gorgeous girl at the gym, the work colleague who always seem to come up smelling of roses or the new woman in your ex's life. You must learn to look at the positive side, the achievements you have made and those that you can make. Set yourself goals, however small, and think 'I can', 'I will' and 'I'll try it' rather than 'I can't', 'Maybe I should have' or 'It's too difficult for me'. If you think you can't do something, then the chances are you won't be able to. If you think there's even a possibility that you can, then you stand a much better chance of success. And even if you don't succeed, you can either try again or dump the thought and at least you'll have learned something about yourself in the process.

The ten key qualities of self-confident people

Self-confident people have around ten key personal qualities. If you feel you need to work on your confidence (to enhance your dating potential!), try adopting some of these principles and make them work for you:

❶ They learn from their mistakes, move on and don't dwell on the past.

❷ They take risks and make calculated decisions knowing that even if they're wrong the results will provide an insight into future risk taking and decision making.

❸ They take up as many new social opportunities as possible.

❹ They have a good understanding of how they can look their best to feel good about themselves.

⑤ They tend to be optimistic – believing that the glass is half-full rather than half-empty.

⑥ They dump emotional baggage as soon as possible and move on without pre-conceived ideas.

⑦ They believe that life is what you make it and anything's possible within reason – they are in control of life rather than letting life control them.

⑧ They also have realistic expectations about life – it isn't always what it's cracked up to be, but that's fine by them.

⑨ They are adept at both giving and receiving compliments.

⑩ They understand and feel comfortable with their own individuality, even if their style appears a little unorthodox to others!

Overcoming shyness

Shyness can be socially crippling. Why does it seem that everyone else has something witty to say, while you feel tongue-tied? And when you do manage to say something, either it never sounds as sharp or as clever as you intended it to or it just comes out the wrong way.

Being shy can make dating seem impossibly daunting. How are you going to get noticed if you don't feel you can communicate or even respond to someone, never mind make the first move? But even shy people can drop subtle hints by returning a smile or maintaining eye contact. And don't be frightened that you'll be laughed at. If that guy you fancy and have just smiled at then turns to his mates and laughs, then he's probably not worth getting to know anyway. It does help to meet people through people you already know, i.e. at parties or at work, rather than a bar. Having something in common from the start is a good icebreaker. A bonus shy people have is that they often make good listeners – or they certainly appear to be good listeners. Shy people also often come across as enigmatic and intriguing. Some guys relish the challenge of shy girls – confidence can be scary and off-putting to some men.

If you've got a date but are worried that you might be tongue-tied, choose an event like a football match or the cinema to go to. The action will restrict the time that you can talk, as well as giving you something to talk about afterwards or during the interval. Asking questions that don't simply require a 'yes' or 'no' answer will enable conversation to flow more easily too, but beware turning the evening into an interrogation! It can be tempting to hurl questions one after the other, without really listening to the answers, just to ensure that there are no embarrassing silences. Good topics that lead to easy-going conversation are work, family, music and hobbies. Where your date was brought up and school or university days are also usually uncomplicated and safe areas to explore.

Preparing for a date is always a good idea. Taking a little time to plan what you are going to wear, will avoid any last minute panic and ensure that you look your very best. And remember, however confident you may think he is, *everybody* is nervous on a first date! Try to relax as much as possible and be yourself. If he wanted to date the life and soul of the party, he wouldn't have asked you out! And if you do feel nervous, anxious, excited or shy there's no harm in saying so (though don't go overboard!) as it is often an endearing trait and curiously will make you and your date feel more at ease and relaxed.

Top tips for overcoming shyness

1. Don't think of yourself as shy – it can have negative connotations. Think of yourself as quiet or a good listener instead.

2. Don't forget those things that you are good at and interested in.

3. Smile, look up and make eye contact.

4. Compliment people and accept compliments with a smile and a thank you.

5. Don't beat yourself up over your shyness – almost all of us experience it at one time or another.

6. Mentally practise awkward situations and try out a pleasant comment or two before you go out to see how it feels.

7. Make small talk as often as possible by talking to shop assistants, the postman and work colleagues.

8. Have a drink before a date – a glass of wine will make you feel more relaxed, but don't have too much.

9. Make sure you look your very best so that you feel comfortable and relaxed in yourself.

Dependency

Most of us have some sort of 'life prop', whether it's tobacco, alcohol, shopping, food or work. The instant 'highs' that these things give us are part of busy, stressful lives. It's only when we relinquish control of our own lives and let these 'props' take over, that we become dependent and play a much more dangerous game. Some people become dependent on other people. They can't imagine life without their partner and will hang on to them at any cost – even if this involves emotional or physical abuse. This is not the place to tackle a serious issue like dependency or how to overcome it, but there is help out there from books or your GP. It is however worth looking at your life and seeing whether you have ever been dependent on a partner, even if only slightly and look again at the questions about self-esteem on page 47. Many dependent people have particularly low self-esteem, often emanating from unhappy childhoods. Dependency is a cycle which has a habit of repeating itself, so if this sounds like you, do think about getting some professional help to regain control before embarking on another relationship.

Sexual self-confidence

One of the reasons that we feel sexier and enjoy love-making more as we get older is related to the higher levels of self-esteem and self-confidence that we often develop as we move out of our teens and twenties. As well as feeling more relaxed in bed, we are more willing to try out new positions and places to make love. Sexual self-confidence allows us to feel lust and passion and be pro-active about making sure that we get what we want; we know what makes us feel good and we know how we can make our partner feel good. Knowing that you can make a man groan with pleasure with a little sensuous foreplay is hugely empowering and rewards you with an increased level of self-confidence. Confidence also helps us feel less stressed and anxious about life in general and both stress and anxiety can be passion killers in the bedroom. If you worry less about the way your own body looks you are free to indulge yourself sexually because you enjoy and deserve it. Having sexual self-confidence can make hedonists and pleasure-seekers out of any of us and sex is one of the areas in life where the pleasure principle is vital to maximum enjoyment.

Being sexually alluring is not just about how much of your cleavage you are showing or wearing a pair of killer heels – sexiness comes from within. Truly sexy people can still look hot in an old jumper and baggy jeans, just as those who don't have sex appeal can end up looking cheap when they wear reveal-ing clothes, rather than become sexy sirens. People who have a good level of self-confidence, who feel comfortable and happy in themselves, tend to be more relaxed, laugh more, be more natural and that can be incredibly sexy, even if they are not conventional beauties. The combination of pride and care in your appearance, natural, unforced behaviour and feeling at ease with your personality and your body is a heady and sexy cocktail. It is also true that most sexy women know that they are sexy and know how best to use it.

Chapter 5

Communication

getting your
message across

Good communication is the key to any successful relationship – whether it's with your colleagues, your family or with your partner. Communication is not simply knowing what to say and when to say it, it is also about listening, understanding and responding to people in the right way. For many people this comes as naturally to them as cleaning their teeth or getting dressed in the morning. They just get on with it. To others, it's a much more daunting prospect altogether and generally related to their own self-esteem and confidence levels (see the previous chapter for more on this).

Effective listening

A healthy level of communication starts with effective listening. That means giving your full attention to your partner. We all lead busy lives and there will always be times when you have to listen to a long-term partner while cooking the dinner or getting dressed, but do try not to have one eye on the TV or on the clock. Keep your eyes on him, focus and try and give him your full attention. Listen and respond effectively or ask a relevant question. There are many well-established couples who have simply lost the ability to listen to each other because they are too busy coping with children, keeping a home together, working hard and maintaining busy social lives. These couples often end up in what is known as the 'empty nest' syndrome – their children grow up and leave home, they retire and they look at each other and wonder what on earth they are going to talk about! What's more, they wonder whether they ever had anything to talk about to start with. Chances are they did at one time. But, we're not too concerned about long-established relationships here – we're looking at meeting people, dating and having that all-important fun! But it's worth remembering that early patterns of good communication can make or break a relationship, especially when the initial 'bonk-til-you-bust' phase has passed and you've settled into a gentler routine.

"Many couples have lost the ability to communicate with each other because they are so busy with children, keeping a home, working hard and maintaining a busy social life."

Effective communication

These joke diary entries reveal how lack of communication coupled with the very different ways that men and women interpret each other can lead to some big – and very unnecessary – misunderstandings. While these diaries are meant to be amusing, how often it happens in real life is a lesson to us all.

GIRL'S DIARY

FRIDAY 21st June 2002
Saw John in the evening and he was acting really strangely. I went shopping in the afternoon with the girls and I did turn up a bit late so I thought it might be that. The bar was really crowded and loud so I suggested we go somewhere quieter to talk. He was still very subdued and distracted so I suggested we go somewhere nice to eat. All through dinner he just didn't seem himself; he hardly laughed, and didn't seem to be paying any attention to me or to what I was saying. I just knew that something was wrong. He dropped me back home and I wondered if he was going to come in; he hesitated, but followed. I asked him again if there was something the matter but he just half shook his head and turned the television on.

After about 10 minutes of silence, I said I was going upstairs to bed. I put my arms around him and told him that I loved him deeply. He just gave a sigh, and a sad sort of smile. He didn't follow me up, but later he did, and I was surprised when we made love. He still seemed distant and a bit cold, and I started to think that he was going to leave me, and that he had found someone else. I cried myself to sleep.

BOY'S DIARY

FRIDAY 21st June 2002
England lost to Brazil 2-1. Got a shag though.

DOS AND DON'TS OF FIRST CONTACT

Do

- **Smile** – It's simple, effective and costs nothing!

- **Listen** – take an interest in what he is saying.

- **Make eye contact** – again simple, effective and very sexy!

- **Make intelligent conversation** – small talk is fine but don't come over as 'ditsy' unless you are actively going for 'bimbo appeal'.

- **Try to laugh in the right places** – it shows that you're listening and amused by what you are hearing. Remember too that the right sort of laugh is both endearing and relaxing. Cackling like a witch is not!

- **Pay compliments** – a little flattery always goes down well.

- **Flirt a little** – it's an invaluable weapon in your dating arsenal.

- **Tease him a little** – it shows you are relaxed and that you have a sense of humour.

- **Make him laugh** – it tells you that he's listening and is finding you attractive and entertaining.

- **Repeat his name at least once** – it's a sign of potential intimacy and, again, it shows that you are listening.

- **Keep a little mystique** – don't tell him your life story all at once, hold a little something back for the next time you meet...

- **Leave him wanting more!**

- **Last but not least** – make him see that meeting up with you again would definitely be a wise move.

Making an approach

So there you are at the party and this to-die-for guy has just returned your bold smile and is now making his way over to you. You've checked behind you to make sure that it's not the leggy brunette he's heading towards, but she seems to be deep in conversation with someone else, so it just has to be you. Okay, clearly as he's making a move towards you he's bound to utter the first word. And that's likely to be 'hi'. And you're going to say 'hi' back.

Don't

• **Whinge or moan** – grumbling about the unbearable heat, loud music or your resulting headache will not make you seem fun.

• **Talk over him or keep interrupting** – it shows disinterest and is rude.

• **Look over his shoulder or down to the floor** – it will make him feel awkward, dull and uncomfortable.

• **Talk about the weather** – unless you're a professional weather reporter, of course. For everyone else, it's just not sexy.

• **Look bored or miserable** – remember to smile!

• **Be rude (not even dirty rude at this stage)** – think about what you are saying. Acerbic wit can often come over as sarcasm during an early encounter.

• **Flirt too much** – unless you've already decided to take him home!

• **Over tease** – he will just feel embarrassed or irritated.

• **Tell a joke** – you're not one of his footie mates or boozing pals.

• **Forget his name or worse still, get it wrong** – if you're not sure about his name, do not try and use something you thought you might have heard or remembered.

• **Tell him everything there is to know about yourself** – however fascinating it might be, he doesn't need to know everything about you yet.

• **Be too eager** – unless he's desperate, he'll head for the hills. Even in the 21st century, men generally like to do most of the pursuing.

Then what? It's best to stick to the tried and tested openers for the first few minutes. The 'Are you a mate of X (insert appropriate host or hostess name here)?' or 'don't you work with X?' are good opening gambits. The brave can go for 'love the shirt' or whatever, but don't go into full flirt mode too fast. If you're in a bar or somewhere else where there is no previous personal connection, you could try something like 'are you local?' instead. Please don't, under any circumstances, say 'do you come here often?' or 'what's a nice guy like you doing in a dump like this?' Both are just too much of cliché

"Even if you're feeling nervous, cheesy chat up lines are not a good idea."

and fall into the same category as the definite no-nos that 'witty' men like to use, such as 'Get your coat, you've pulled' or 'Nice dress. It would look even better on my bedroom floor'! Even when you're feeling nervous, cheesy chat up lines are not a good idea, unless you're 'Speed Dating' of course (for more on this, see page 156), when time is short and it becomes ironic and therefore acceptable!

Needless to say, every situation needs to be (quickly) assessed and judged on it's own merits, but these few cautionary 'do's and don'ts' might help you. Of course, if you suddenly realize that you've made a mistake and that the cute guy is not quite as cute close up or that he's simply not for you, just employ a few elements of the 'don'ts' list and you should achieve the desired effect!

Are you a good communicator?

Ask yourself the following questions. Be honest. Or better still, ask a close friend to answer these questions of *your* communication skills.

1. Would you describe your/my level of communication as:
A Healthy – you find it easy to express yourself, are generally understood and usually know when to listen and when to talk.
B Okay – you are always the life and soul of any social occasion but don't always let other people have their say.
C Reluctant – you tend not to volunteer information, unless asked a direct question, and you then find it difficult to express your feelings.

2. Would you describe your/my listening skills as:
A Excellent – you enjoy listening to what other people have to say, even if their views differ from your own.
B Okay – you listen if you need to but if you disagree or have something to say, you usually butt in with your views.
C Good – you'd much rather let other people talk anyway.

3. If someone close to you is upset about something, what's your reaction:
A Take time out to listen, try to understand and where possible make some practical suggestions for ways of coping with the problem.
B Tell them to pull themselves together, have a drink and forget about it. Tomorrow is another day.
C Try to avoid talking about it, as you often don't know what to say or how to make them feel better.

4. When you are making plans to go out for a night out with a friend, do you tend to:

A Talk it over and come up with somewhere that suits you both, even if it's not your ideal venue.

B Know and suggest the perfect place. They'll love it.

C Submit happily to wherever she wants to go, as you really don't have an opinion about it.

5. He's gorgeous, but he's talking about football – what do you do? You want to hold his attention:

A Smile and tell him that footie's not really your thing, but what is the big joke about the offside rule? Explain pleeease…

B Tell him the only thing that you like about football are the player's thighs and change the subject swiftly.

C Listen and nod occasionally. You are not really interested but anyway you don't feel strongly one way or another.

6. You are on a first date. It's all going well, he's going to drop you home and you know he wants to be invited in, but you definitely do not want to have sex with him. Do you:

A Invite him in for that coffee but make it clear in the nicest possible way that while a snog might be on the menu, a three-course meal definitely isn't.

B Tell him you don't 'do' sex on a first date, so if he thinks you're that kind of girl he can take a hike!

C See if he asks to come in and if he does, just let him. Make that coffee and see what he wants to do. You don't want to appear rude.

Scores

Mainly 'A'
You need a little more practice or maybe an occasional pause for thought is all that's required.

Mainly 'B'
Take a long look at your past relationships, current friendships and general approach to life – it may be that you're in danger of trying to run the show single-handedly.

Mainly 'C'
You need to revisit basic communication skills and overcome your reluctance to speak up for yourself.

Communication after the first date

This is a really thorny issue and while no one can really say what's best in individual situations, I can give you a little sound advice that's based on my own experience and that of a number of my girlfriends over many years.

It's one of those situations that should be so straightforward. Hey, aren't we all living in the 21st century? You sleep with a guy on the first date – or even the first meeting – if it feels right and you don't if it doesn't. You are in control, you enjoy spending time with men and have every right to call them if you want to see them again. So you don't sit by the phone waiting for it to ring – you ring or text him. Great. While all of this is true, it is also a fact that the fundamental differences between men and women always rear their ugly (and predictable) heads at times like these... You can read more about the differences between men and women in Chapter 7: Venus and Mars, but I'd like to highlight a few basics here. And yes, they are bloody infuriating, but arming yourself with this information will make the whole dating game that much easier to handle. I'm not saying that all of the following points are true for all men, all of the time, but experience tells me that unless they tell you something to the contrary, you won't go too far wrong if you accept the home truths on pages 61–4.

So what does that little lot really mean when it comes to contacting a man after a first date? Most importantly, it means that you should *never* contact a man after the first date if you have had sex with him. If it was a one-night stand, then calling him will make little difference and if it wasn't, then he'll call you. It's one of those intractable rules that I loathe as much as many of you will, but I have never known it to be a sensible or productive move.

If you didn't sleep with him and you don't want to wait for him to call, give it at least two days before contacting him (but no longer than four days, or he'll think you have been waiting for him to call and are now getting desperate...). And even then I'd suggest a friendly text or email along the lines of 'I had a great time the other night, hope all is well with you' or something similar. Then you've paved the way but have let him think he's taken the next crucial step. Occasionally it's appropriate to send a text on the same evening – especially if he's got a long jopurney home – 'thanks for a fun evening' or 'have a safe journey' are both quite acceptable and show that you are a decent, caring person too!

If you do decide to call him, make sure that you're sober, relaxed and not likely to be interrupted. If you get his answer-phone or voicemail then just leave a friendly message but don't ask him to call you back. If you hang up without leaving a message he's is quite likely to do a '1471' or 'last caller' on his phone. Even men learnt something from *Bridget Jones's Diary* you know!

Once you're a few dates down the line, the whole situation becomes that much more relaxed and you'll be able to gauge whether calling him is a good idea or not much more easily.

Men like to make the first move
In their testosterone-fuelled fantasies, men dream of beautiful, busty blondes coming on strong to them, while they are powerless to resist. She makes her move, barely speaks, beckons him over and off they go to her penthouse flat and make wild passionate love all night on her silk sheets while she enjoys every minute of his perfect performance. She expects nothing more than to give him pleasure and receive his with moans of delight. While this is undoubtedly the ultimate fantasy – and most men appreciate it as such – there's a vestige of alpha male in most men that sees any woman making the first move as a direct and rapid invitation into bed. They think that they were born to make the selection and make the moves. Some more liberated men don't think this way of course, but the vast majority still do I'm afraid.

Men expect to do the pursuing
This is really just an extension of the above. In the early days of dating, they expect to be the ones to make the running even if they're quite happy for you to pay half the expenses! Once a relationship is more established, this expectation changes and it becomes more acceptable for you to call or text him to arrange the next date. This will change over the course of time, but sadly it is the still the expectation of most men.

Men panic when women are too keen
Of course you can be keen in bed, but if there's the slightest whiff of your taking the relationship too fast, too soon, then men will often feel trapped, threatened and ultimately disempowered.

Men like to believe they're in control, even if it's clear to you they're not
During the course of the last generation women have increasingly stolen the traditional man's thunder – we take their jobs, their earning power and their emotional independence. While they may accept this – reluctantly or other-wise – many men believe that it is the traditional role of men to have the upper hand in a relationship, to show who wears the trousers. Even if you earn more than him, have a bigger house or a better car, again the alpha male kicks in during a relationship and they like to feel that they are in control. Much of the time they are not of course – we girls know that – but it does no harm to pander to this vestige of male pride, if you want to sus-tain the relationship.

Words women use...breaking the code!

The following mock 'glossary' amused me. It's clearly written by a man for men (anonymous unfortunately, but my grateful thanks go to him) to help decipher some of the words and signals we women use and the way in which we use them. Entertaining yes, but perhaps there's more than a grain of truth in it?

Fine. This is the word we use at the end of any argument that we feel we are right about but need to shut her up. *Never* use 'fine' to describe how a woman looks. This will cause you to have one of *those* arguments.

Five Minutes. This is half an hour. It is equivalent to the five minutes that your football game is going to last before you take out the rubbish, so it's a fair trade.

Nothing. This means something and you should be on your toes. 'Nothing' is usually used to describe the feeling that a woman has of wanting to turn you inside out, upside down and backwards. 'Nothing' usually signifies an argument that will last 'five minutes' and end with the word 'fine'.

Go Ahead (with raised eyebrows). This is a dare. One that will result in a woman getting upset over 'nothing' and will end with the word 'fine'.

Go Ahead (with normal eyebrows). This means 'I give up' or 'do what you want because I don't care'. You will get a 'go ahead' with raised eyebrow in just a few minutes, followed by 'nothing' and 'fine' and she will talk to you in about 'five minutes' when she cools off.

Men take things at face value, while women look for a deeper meaning
What do you do on a girlie night out? Look at the blokes in the bar, thinking 'phwoar' or 'no way'? Yes, but we also put the world to rights with our girlfriends. Endlessly analyze and seek advice on relationships. We seek reassurance from them and talk the close ones through every developing step of the way, especially in the early days or when we sense something might be wrong. What do men do? Look at the girls in the bar, go 'phwoar'

Loud Sigh. This is not technically a word, but is still a verbal statement often misunderstood by men. A loud sigh means that she thinks you are an idiot at that moment and wonders why she is wasting her time standing here and arguing with you over 'nothing'.

Soft Sigh. Again not a word but a verbal statement nonetheless. Soft sighs are one of the few things that men actually understand. She is content. Your best bet is to not to move or breathe and she will stay that way.

That's Okay. This is one of the most dangerous statements that a woman can say to a man. 'That's okay' means that she wants to think long and hard before paying you retributions for whatever it is that you have done. 'That's okay' is often used with the word 'fine' and used in conjunction with a raised eyebrow 'go ahead'. At some point in the not too distant future, when she has had time to plot and plan, you will be in big trouble.

Please Do. Not a statement but an offer. A woman is giving you the chance to come up with whatever excuse or reason you have for doing whatever it is that you have done. You have a fair chance to tell the truth, so be careful and you shouldn't get a 'That's okay'.

Thanks. A woman is thanking you. Do not faint – just say 'you're welcome'.

Thanks A Lot. This is very different from 'thanks'. A woman will say 'thanks a lot' when she is really pissed off with you. It signifies that you have hurt her in some callous way and will be followed by the 'loud sigh'. Be careful not to ask her what is wrong after the 'loud sigh', as she will only tell you 'nothing'.

and then go on to discuss football, beer and the size of the tits of the third one on the right, just to left of the pillar. Enough said…

Men find strong, assertive women as sexy as they find them scary
Men love strong, sassy, bright women with a sharp and dry sense of humour. They're bound to be great fun in bed. Being so sorted and independent, they may not want a relationship beyond the bedroom. And even if they do,

they're probably too demanding and opinionated for them. The sweeter, kinder, softer version of womanhood is much nicer to go out with ultimately. They're so much more grateful and less demanding. Sounds bullshit? I agree, but it's a rough paraphrase of something a sane, intelligent, eligible bloke told me, someone who really ought to know better but represents men the entire world over...

Men invented the phrase 'one-night stand'
The one-night stand fulfils a basic sexual need for men and most can walk away emotionally unscathed. Do you know many women who go out on the pull for the night, see and approach a cutie, get him pissed, take him home, shag his brains out and say goodbye in the morning without a second thought? Yeah, I know we've all watched 'Ibiza Uncovered' or similar, but generally we're after a little more than that. Our sexual needs are greater than a physical ache that needs to be relieved and, most of us don't sort blokes out into those that might be hot in bed and those that we might want to date. Shock horror – we want both in one package, and quite rightly don't see why we can't hold out for that dating nirvana.

Chapter 6

Compatibility

a match made
in heaven?

Compatibility is important in any relationship. But what makes us compatible with someone else? What is that elusive, hard to define quality that we look for in every man we meet? Usually, we know when we find it in someone. But what, exactly, does that person have that we need? What is it that makes us compatible?

Chemistry

Chemistry is enormously hard to define. It's not as simple as whether you fancy a man or not. It is a primeval attraction that seems to spring from nowhere the instant you first encounter someone. It is one of the most essential elements of any relationship and while having good chemistry between you is no guarantee of a successful relationship, a relationship without any chemistry is almost certainly doomed from the start.

"You can grow to love someone, you can even grow to fancy someone, but chemistry is either there from the outset or it's not."

You can grow to love someone, you can even grow to fancy someone, but chemistry is either there from the outset or it's not. It may be a mixture of things about him – his eyes, the way he smiles or moves his hands when he talks. It may be his six-pack, the back of his neck or his ability to make you laugh. But it won't be his bank balance, his flashy job or his love of sailing, it's far less definable and material, that's for sure. It's sometimes what attracts us to bad boys and can make even the most unsuitable men very hard to resist once it kicks in. It gives you butterflies in the pit of your stomach, makes your head spin and can give you the highest of highs. It's like lust at first sight and when it happens it can take your breath away. It's dangerous, wonderful, powerful and frankly, it's scary, because it's hard to control your feelings, even if you are just about able to control what you actually do about them.

As I've already said, it's not completely about his looks either. You can find yourself enormously attracted to someone who defies all your preconceived ideas about what you find attractive. He's definitely not a conventional head turner, but you're blushing at his every word, you feel anxious, wobbly and ever so slightly out of control. It happens fast and with a passion. To hell with convention and your personal rule book! You just want to get his clothes off and get down to it. The only trouble is, it can happen when you meet your best friend's new boyfriend, the window cleaner or your new boss. Reason then has to kick in or there's big trouble afoot! But if it happens when you meet someone who is unattached and who is clearly attracted to you too, then harness all that delicious passion and lust and just enjoy!

Chemistry, combined with other powerful feelings that exist *outside* the bedroom, is the headiest combination in the world and well worth hanging on to if you find it in a relationship. Chemistry rarely wanes – unlike plain old lust – and if you find you get on with him just as well when you're out with a crowd of mates or just staying in watching TV, you may just have an enduring and enviable relationship on your hands! And controversial though my view probably is, I'm a firm believer that a good, lasting relationship can come out of that initial chemistry, even if all the other compatibility factors, like looks, common goals, social status etc. aren't necessarily there. A strong and enduring sexual passion often justifies making more compromises on other fronts so be less demanding *outside* of the bedroom and just go with the flow. And hey, if it doesn't work out, you've had a fantastic time between the sheets! If the chemistry's not there, despite that fact that you get on like a house on fire, you probably don't have an enduring relationship that is going to work out. What you've got is a potentially great friend.

Looks

There is no denying that looks are important. They are the first thing that we see and what forms our initial impression as to whether we fancy someone or not. It's not necessarily down to how good-looking someone is, but is often about how confident or relaxed someone seems or whether they are well groomed or well presented. A black polo-necked jumper on an average-looking man will always look better than a beer-stained rugby shirt on a handsome man. Of course it's easier for women to look good. There are a lot of cosmetic enhancements out there to help us – hair colours, well-applied make-up and Lycra hold-it-all-ins can make a big difference to how we look. What these things also give us is the confidence that comes from knowing that we look good and that, in turn, makes us more appealing to men.

Men do not have access to quite so many props. Well, they do I suppose, but a man with permed, highlighted hair or 'lifts' in his shoes just comes over as a bit sad. It's an unfair world, but that's the way it is. Many men don't think that they have to make any effort at all to look good but nice teeth, a sexy smile, clean clothes and a little effort on the beer belly front go a long way to making a man more appealing to women.

Generally speaking, the beautiful people of this world end up with beautiful partners and the plain people with plain ones. It's not always so, of course, and there should always be more to any relationship than just looks – but it does help to have realistic expectations. We might have the hots for Tom Cruise or George Clooney, but it would be foolish and ultimately disappointing to be seeking to date a carbon copy of either of them.

Looks *do* matter, whether we like it or not. He may be bright, witty, kind and ambitious, but if he doesn't do it in the looks department for you and you don't actually fancy him, it's not a promising start. Thank god, we are not all after exactly the same type of man! I'm a great believer in going for a man who isn't the best looking in the room. Men who are not quite so good looking tend to try harder (they have to!) and can't take their looks for granted. Going out with a seriously handsome man can make you feel quite anxious. The head-turner who makes every woman look around when he walks in to a room can make a girl feel very insecure.

Sex Appeal

There's something slightly old-fashioned about the expression 'sex appeal'. If someone has sex appeal it means other people find them sexy, but often it's not because of their looks alone. Seriously beautiful people can often lack sex appeal, while other, seemingly less attractive people are often deemed to be very sexy indeed. It's also not about how much cleavage or leg a woman displays or how much a man struts about in thong swimwear or ball-crushing trousers! It's got much more to do with being natural and knowing what makes you look good, holding your head high, smiling – all of these can be sexy. So can vulnerability, shyness or just looking relaxed and friendly. Sex appeal is also very much in the eye of the beholder.

Someone who you think has sex appeal means, in its purest sense, that they look like the kind of person that you would want to have sex with. Someone who would give and take pleasure in equal amounts and be good for you in bed. But remember, we live in a competitive world and you might sometimes feel that in order to have the edge over another women you will have to make yourself look more 'available'. This isn't necessarily the case. It's better to know what makes you look good and keep a little something under wraps. Showing a glimpse of thigh is a whole lot sexier than wearing a too-short skirt. And it's the same for men. A touch of gel to keep wayward locks in place is far cuter than hair covered in a tub of grease, just as the outline of a well-honed bicep in a white T-shirt is generally more attractive than a nipple through a string vest! Sex appeal owes a lot to mystery and the allure of possibility. It's comes from being confident, listening, looking and adding just a hint of flirty promise in the right places. It's not cheesy chat-up lines and a ton of over-powering after-shave…

It's a common belief that you either have sex appeal or you don't. It's true that you can't manufacture it or have cosmetic surgery to enhance it. But everybody is capable of being sexy to someone else although, just like chemistry, it may be elusive at times. You can be sure that when you find someone where your level of sex appeal is mutual, it can be electric. If you enjoy sex and like people you're far more likely to appear sexy to someone else than if you try to look cool and disinterested.

There is a degree of similarity in what makes a man or a woman sexy to each other. These are just a few factors that make someone sexy:

Sexy people are not fixated on their looks – women who constantly reapply their lipstick or men who constantly check themselves out in the mirror to ensure there's not a hair out of place, are not sexy. Tousled hair can be really sexy – it reminds people of that 'just got out of bed' look.

Sexy people are comfortable with their looks – they sit naturally, look relaxed and don't try and hide their stomachs, noses or whatever. They've already dressed in the way that they know shows them at their best.

Sexy people are fun – they have infectious enthusiasm, know how to enjoy themselves and smile a lot.

Sexy people are interested in other people – they listen and participate in a group because they want to, not because it will pass the time or they feel obliged. They make other people feel important and special.

Sexy people believe in themselves – they may be controversial at times, but they are never dull. They have the confidence to stick to their beliefs but the humility to listen to other viewpoints.

Sexy people are tactile – they enjoy brushing an arm, touching a hand, and kissing hello. They're not touchy-feely in a creepy way, just warm, affectionate and open.

Sexy people know the power of eye contact – they can say more with their eyes than with words. They can hold your eyes just a moment longer than is normally acceptable, without holding it so long that they cause you any embarrassment.

How compatible are you?

There are certain issues, whether we are aware of them or not, that dictate compatibility. Our culture, interests, political views, class, religion, education, career choice, background and income level all indicate compatibility. While we may not be actively seeking partners who are mirror images of ourselves, it is certainly easier to make a successful relationship with someone with whom you at least share a little common ground. Unless you are genuinely ready, willing and able to compromise – or your partner is – then a lack of common ground is likely to have an impact after the initial period of infatuation wears off. Serious incompatibility will often show up early on in a relationship. If you hate swearing, prejudice of any kind, ethnic food, smoking or clubbing and your date exhibits these tendencies, then you're going to become aware that you are fundamentally incompatible pretty quickly. So, if politics are important to you and you couldn't possibly consider dating someone who votes Tory, then check this out early on. Ditto if you loathe smoking and couldn't bear to kiss a smoker, for example.

The next stage when signs of potential incompatibility can reveal themselves comes a few weeks into the relationship, when the initial phase of trying to impress each other is giving way to a more relaxed style. If his behaviour starts to change at this point, then it's likely that the real him is emerging and, despite a promising start, you may be incompatible! For example:

Signs of incompatibility

• He used to buy you dinner, send flowers and ring whenever the mood took him, but now he has stopped.

• He was always punctual and if he was going to be a little late, he would text you to say so, but now he's always late and he never lets you know.

• His once impressively clean and tidy flat, has become a cesspit of empty beer bottles, take-away cartons and unwashed underwear.

• The car door that was opened for you has become a thing of the past.

• His moderate drinking of good white wine has become six pints of beer.

If all/any of these things start to happen he has probably slipped into what I call 'normal complacency'. Once you've managed to get through the first month or two and nothing startlingly untoward has happened, life will seem a lot more relaxed. It might not indicate a lifetime of compatibility – that can take years – but at least you're probably not in for any major incompatibility surprises.

A COMPATIBILITY TEST

Think about the following statements. They will help you to find out whether you're likely to be compatible with your new man. These points are (in no particular order of priority) some of the common goals that bind people together beyond the initial stages of a relationship. It is important to share at least half of these if you want to go beyond the first date.

- Looks are/are not that important to me.
- I have a high/low sex drive.
- It's important/not important that we share political views.
- I love/am not bothered about dining out.
- I hate/don't mind smoking.
- I hate/don't mind drinking.
- I am/am not a party animal.
- I am/am not ambitious.
- Household chores should be/don't need to be shared.
- I believe/don't believe in fidelity.
- I'm looking for/not looking for a serious commitment at the moment.
- I want/don't want children.
- I would like/am not bothered about being with someone who has achieved the same level of educational as me.
- I need/do not need to be with someone of the same religion as me.
- I like/don't like/don't mind tattoos or piercings.
- I like/don't like the outdoor life.
- It is important/not important to me that someone shares my interests.
- I prefer going out/staying in.
- I want someone who is/is not romantic.
- I want a man who is/is not practical.
- I like/don't like spontaneity or surprises.

Using star signs to assess compatibility

I'm not a devotee of determining compatibility via the stars, though I must admit to holding a sneaky belief in astrology and I always enjoy reading my own horoscope. I know that many people truly believe that there is something significant in star signs though and so, just for them, here's a potted version of how it all works. Have fun with it, use it wisely but don't take it too seriously!

Astrological sun signs fall into four elements, Earth, Fire, Air and Water. The general belief is that a relationship with someone within the same element as you i.e. Gemini and Libra (Air) or Virgo and Capricorn (Earth) will work better than one with someone from a different group, such as Pisces and Leo (Water and Fire) or Aquarius and Taurus (Air and Earth). However Fire and Earth signs can work well together, as can Air and Water. Fire and Water are not meant to be compatible (Fire does turns Water to steam after all!) nor are Fire and Air (Fire consumes Air...), Earth and Water (Earth dams Water) and Earth and Air (which is just not very exciting apparently!).

Which sign are you?
Earth
TAURUS – April 20th to May 20th

VIRGO – August 23rd to September 22nd

CAPRICORN – December 22nd to January 19th

Fire
ARIES – March 21st to April 19th

LEO – July 23rd to August 22nd

SAGITTARIUS – November 22nd to December 21st

Air
GEMINI – May 21st to June 20th

LIBRA – September 23rd to October 22nd

AQUARIUS – January 20th to February 18th

Water
CANCER – June 21st to July 22nd

SCORPIO – October 23rd to November 21st

PISCES – February 19th to March 20th

Which signs are you compatible with?

Now you know your own sign, you can figure out how compatible you are likely to be with your new date. While I don't suggest that you take this too seriously, you may be surprised at just how well this works.

Earth signs: Taurus, Virgo, Capricorn

Earth signs tend to be practical and concerned with material comfort and security. Looks are often important to earth signs, as are 'grounded' people.

Taurus

Most compatible with: Leo, Capricorn, Virgo, Libra and another Taurus
Least compatible with: Gemini, Sagittarius and Aquarius

Virgo

Most compatible with: Pisces, Scorpio, Taurus and Capricorn
Least compatible with: Aries, Libra, Cancer, Aquarius, Leo and another Virgo

Capricorn

Most compatible with: Scorpio, Aquarius, Taurus, Virgo, Leo and another Capricorn
Least compatible with: Libra, Gemini, Sagittarius, and Aries

Fire signs: Aries, Leo, Sagittarius

Fire signs tend to be active, dynamic and assertive. Passionate and inspired, they are impressed by success and ambition.

Aries

Most compatible with: Scorpio, Leo, Sagittarius, Libra and another Aries
Least compatible with: Cancer, Pisces, Capricorn and Virgo

Leo

Most compatible with: Gemini, Aries, Libra, Taurus, Sagittarius and Capricorn
Least compatible with: Scorpio, Virgo, Aquarius and another Leo

Sagittarius

Most compatible with: Aries, Leo, Gemini, and another Sagittarius
Least compatible with: Capricorn, Taurus, Cancer, Aquarius, Scorpio, Libra and Pisces

Air signs: Gemini, Libra, Aquarius

Air signs are energetic and logical. A meeting of minds is often as important as someone's looks.

Gemini

Most compatible with: Libra, Leo, Aquarius and Sagittarius
Least compatible with: Cancer, Capricorn, Taurus, Pisces, and Scorpio

Libra

Most compatible with: Aquarius, Aries, Pisces, Gemini, Leo, Scorpio and Taurus
Least compatible with: Capricorn, Cancer, Virgo, and another Libra

Aquarius

Most compatible with: Libra, Gemini, Capricorn and another Aquarius
Least compatible with: Scorpio, Taurus, Virgo, Leo, Sagittarius, Pisces, and Cancer

Water signs: Cancer, Scorpio, Pisces

Water signs are emotional and intuitive. While they respect their own privacy – and that of others – they also love both passion and loyalty.

Cancer

Most compatible with: Pisces, Scorpio and another Cancer
Least compatible with: Sagittarius, Libra, Gemini, Virgo, Aquarius and Aries

Scorpio

Most compatible with: Pisces, Aries, Cancer, Virgo, Capricorn and Libra
Least compatible with: Gemini, Sagittarius, Leo, Aquarius and another Scorpio

Pisces

Most compatible with: Libra, Scorpio, Virgo, Cancer and another Pisces
Least compatible with: Sagittarius, Aquarius, Gemini and Aries

venus
and
mars

what are the real differences
between the sexes?

Back in 1992, an American lecturer and relationship counsellor, John Gray, wrote the phenomenal best-seller *Men are from Mars, Women are from Venus*. It is subtitled 'The Definitive Guide to Relationships', and the book is now considered to be a modern classic. Basically, it looks at differences between the sexes and highlights the contrasting ways in which men and women interpret the world. By pin-pointing these dissimilarities, the author aims to show that we can have much better relationships if we take the time and trouble to acknowledge, understand and appreciate the differences between the sexes.

I can't argue with his basic premise – clearly there are major differences between the sexes and in the main that's a good thing. But I do think it's wrong to categorize everyone in the same way. I know – as I'm sure you do – a number of women who could quite happily fit into the male 'Mars' group and a fair number of men whose personalities would make them more of a 'Venus'! The fundamental point, though, is that we are all individuals and products of our upbringing (nurture), our inherited genes (nature) plus a whole welter of other stuff (both good and bad) that life throws at us and we develop into unique, individuals irrespective of our gender.

However, there *are* some fundamental differences and it's worth outlining some of them here, along with just a little guidance on how to work *with* rather than *against* these differences when dating.

Dating

I sometimes think of looking for a date in the same way that I think of going shopping. I love making plans with a girlfriend to go on a shopping trip. I look forward to it as a treat. A couple of hours shopping, then we stop for a chat and a coffee or a glass of wine and then we set off again. We look at the clothes, comment on what we think might suit the other one, ask advice on what something looks like when it's on or whether it would suit us. And, even if at the end of the day neither of us has actually bought a thing, we will still have had a good day out. Looking for a suitable date is just like that except you are shopping for a man instead! It's great if you can find the perfect man who suits you, it's okay if you can find someone who looks good, but turns out to be not quite what you were after, but it is by no means the end of the world if you go home empty-handed. It was a fun night out anyway wasn't it? Just as you have your favourite shops, so you should also try and establish your favourite watering-holes or other potential man-shopping places, as well.

Men tend to loathe shopping. Not all of them do of course – but the majority of red-blooded, heterosexual men would rather have a rabid lion pull rings out of their nipples than go on a shopping trip of any kind. Some will make the effort, of course. We've all seen them looking uncomfortable and shifty outside the changing rooms, nervously waiting for their girlfriend or wife to come out and ask them their opinion. Most mumble that 'it looks great' just to be able to get out of the shop quickly. They find it extraordinary that, even after we've found the 'perfect' dress, we still want to carry on shopping, just to see what else might be around. If they need a jumper, they just visit one or maybe two shops, and then they buy one. They certainly don't shop for the pleasure of shopping itself. And they are much the same when looking for a date. They go out, see someone they fancy, chat her up, pull if they get lucky and take her home if they get luckier still. They know what they want and they just go out and get it.

"When men look for a date, they tend to go out, see someone they fancy, chat her up, pull if they get lucky and take her home if they get luckier still. They know what they want and they just go out and get it."

Though, I have to say that men have definitely become more conniving of late, when dating, not least because we women have sussed out their simple tricks to woo us into bed at the earliest possible stage. This has meant that men have had to develop new and subtler strategies for overcoming our resitance. One of the current favourites is for a man to delay his move until the second date. So, what he does is to ask a woman out on a date and, at the end of the evening when they've had a great time and she's waiting for the 'move', he merely kisses her on the cheek, says thanks for a terrific evening and goes home alone. She's left wondering what she did wrong and why did-n't he at least *try* to get her into bed? She thinks that maybe he didn't fancy her after all. But this man's no fool. He invites her out again and, when her guard is down, he makes his move on his by now slightly confused date, and eureka, he's scored!

While there are a number of these more sophisticated strategies around, the following is a more typical example of what happens on a first date. Doubtless you'll be familiar with the woman's view of the date.

The male's eye view of the first date

❶ I've asked her out.

❷ We're meeting at 8.00pm at the local bar.

❸ If it goes well, we'll grab a bite to eat on the way home.

❹ With a bit of luck we'll have sex on the first date.

❺ I'll see how it goes after that.

THE 'ALTERNATIVE' RULES

The Rules is the most successful dating book ever published. It basically tells women how to behave in order to find and keep a husband and sets out clear 'Rules' that must be followed to the letter. It was serious in intent, chock full of psychobabble and extremely controversial!

As an antidote, I present you with the following light-hearted and amusing version of *The Rules*. Although it's clearly meant to entertain, it contains more than a grain of truth. My thanks go to the anonymous and very perceptive author!

Learn to work the toilet seat. You're a big girl. If it's up, put it down. We need it up, you need it down. You don't hear us complaining about you leaving it down.

Sunday = sports. It's like the full moon or the changing of the tides. Let it be.

Shopping is not a sport. And no, we are never going to think of it that way.

Crying is blackmail.

Ask for what you want. Let us be clear on this one: subtle hints do not work! Strong hints do not work! Obvious hints do not work! Just say it!

'Yes' and 'No' are perfectly acceptable answers to every question.

Come to us with a problem only if you want help solving it. That's what we do. Sympathy is what your girlfriends are for.

Anything we said six months ago is inadmissible in an argument. In fact, all comments become null and void after seven days.

If you won't dress like the Victoria's Secret girls, don't expect us to act like soap opera guys.

The female's eye view of the first date

❶ He's asked me out. What shall I wear? I wonder what kind of things he's interested in talking about? Shall I look sexy and do the leather 'n' lace thing? Or shall I go for demure and less available?

❷ What I shall I drink? White wine – even though I get pissed after three glasses? Or maybe I should have Vodka and Orange – I can drink more of that without getting silly. Why that bar? I wonder if he has taken previous girlfriends there before?

If you think you are fat, you probably are. Don't ask us.

If something we said can be interpreted two ways, and one of the ways makes you sad or angry, we meant the other one.

You can ask us to do something or tell us how you want it done. Not both. If you already know best how to do it, just do it yourself.

Whenever possible, please say whatever you have to say during commercial breaks.

Christopher Columbus did not need directions and neither do we.

All men see in only 16 colours, like Windows default settings. Peach, for example, is a fruit – not a colour. Pumpkin is also a fruit. We have no idea what Mauve is.

If it itches, it will be scratched. We do that.

If we ask what is wrong and you say 'nothing' we will act like nothing's wrong. We know you are lying, but it is just not worth the hassle.

If you want to ask a question you don't want an answer to, expect an answer you don't want to hear.

Don't ask us what we're thinking about unless you are prepared to discuss such topics as football, beer, girls and sex.

You have enough clothes.

You have too many shoes.

Beer is as exciting for us as handbags are for you.

I am in shape. Round is a shape.

❸ Where will we be eating? Has he booked a restaurant? What kind of food? I wonder what time for? Should I eat before I go in case he hasn't booked? It will soak up the alcohol anyway. Shall I offer to pay my share?

❹ Should I sleep with him? What will he expect? How far should I go? Should I ask him in for a coffee? Will he see this as an invitation to have sex? Shall I wear my best underwear in case? Will he have a condom ?

❺ How cool should I be? How do I let him know that this just might be a proper relationship, rather than a casual one nighter? Should I have sex with him? Will this make me look seriously interested or just loose?

Communication

If I had to say what the biggest difference between the sexes is, then it would have to be in our way of communicating. I'd much rather judge people by their individuality rather than by their gender, as I've said previously, but I have to admit that there are major differences here. In essence women tend to look for – and often find – a deeper meaning in many conversations, while men tend to take things at face value.

As you get to know someone, your level of communication naturally increases. Even if your man is not brilliant at expressing himself and chooses to shut himself away after a stressful day, you will learn to recognize that this is because he actually did have a stressful day and it's not because it's anything you did or said! Nor is he now secretly shagging that girl from Accounts, who he said was cute.

In good relationships, couples learn how to communicate with each other and give their partner space when it's needed, rather than bombard each other with questions to get to the bottom of a problem in an instant. They also look at the whole range of methods of communication – not just the spoken word. They recognize subtle body language and pick up changes in mood. This explains why many women get a hunch that their partner is having an affair long before anything tangible like lipstick on his collar or a carelessly discarded restaurant bill make their appearance. It's a shift in mood, body language or tone of voice that they don't recognize and which alerts them to the possibility of a problem.

When men talk to someone – usually a male pal, sometimes their partner – about a problem, they tend to be seeking answers and practical advice. Women will often talk about a problem, just to express how they are feeling and have the emotional release of talking about it. We are not necessarily looking for answers – we are looking for empathy and emotional support. Women often feel that men don't really listen to them. This is because men

THE WAY WE COMMUNICATE

Let's look at the basic differences between the ways in which men and women communicate.

Women tend to:

• Analyze relationships and look for deeper meanings in what's being said to them.

• Notice when someone's troubled – even when nothing has been said.

• Feel more comfortable about expressing their emotions.

• Plan ahead in relationships.

• Express sympathetic concern for a colleague or a friend with relative ease.

• Talk about their personal problems.

• Communicate their feelings in metaphors and with depth.

• Talk about their feelings, about other people and discuss office politics.

• Think out loud.

• Talk more than men but still make better listeners.

Men tend to:

• Take what's being said to them at face value.

• Be oblivious to someone else's problem until it's spelled out for them.

• Find it difficult to express emotions, although they can be quick to show anger.

• Take relationships one day at a time.

• Give practical advice rather than show emotional solidarity.

• Deal with problems by themselves.

• Speak literally – i.e. they call a spade a spade.

• Talk about sport, business and gadgets rather than feelings.

• Keep schtum.

• Interrupt conversations to voice their point of view.

simply aren't used to offering emotional support, so they tend to say nothing. This silence is often mistaken for lack of interest, but it's simply being unfamiliar with knowing what to say, so if in doubt, they say nowt!

Try asking your man for advice. What would he do in the circumstances? What would he say in that situation? Men feel much more comfortable being asked direct questions and will feel much more involved in what's going on. Even if their advice is not what you want to follow at least you will know that the message has been received and understood.

Misunderstanding Body Language

As well as differences in the way that men and women communicate, there are immediately apparent differences in the body language that they use, too. This is due in part to culture, clothing and the way we are physically put together. It is unusual to see a woman slumped in a chair with her legs wide open, for pretty obvious reasons! Just as a man who sits bolt upright with his shoulders back and legs crossed is often viewed as rather camp! Women use body language – either inadvertently or deliberately – to express interest, emotion, keenness or disinterest. We girls can also use it to great effect when flirting (see Chapters 8 and 9 for more guidance on this). Men tend to use body language to enhance their power and to assert themselves. Again, this may or may not be deliberate.

Problems often occur in the way men interpret a woman's body language. Often it's a simple case of wishful thinking on their part, but nevertheless it can cause serious misunderstandings. For instance, if a woman is in full 'flirt mode' and is clearly finding a man interesting and fun, he will often perceive this as a clear signal to make a further, more intimate move. The woman concerned is actually only trying to be flattering and charming and not actually suggesting that the next move is towards the bedroom! Also, when a woman is dancing her heart out with a man and moving rhythmically and sexily to the music, he may see this as a direct signal to move in for a kiss. Often, she is just carried away with the music and enjoying herself. We can feel relaxed enough with a man to let him drive us home, invite him in for that coffee and enjoy a kiss and a little more intimacy before bidding him goodnight. That's a fun evening, right? We can go to bed on our own, knowing that we had a great time and that we are looking forward to seeing him again. While some men accept this, others see it as being a cheat, a tease or a let down, i.e. 'she seemed well up for it, then she said no!' It's a tough and potentially hazardous world out there for men – and they often think that they are at the finishing post when they haven't even left the starting blocks…

Misinterpretation of body language can be something of a conundrum and I'm afraid that it's trial and error and depends a great deal on the maturity and experience of the guy. There's no real way around the situation and if he simply can't accept what's being offered, just stick to your guns, do what feels right and never let yourself give in to his expectations, simply because he thinks you've led him on. You haven't. You both had a good time, you enjoyed a snog or two and you've given him the green light for another date, when you may or may not put out!

<table>
<tr><td>

He needs:

- Admiration
- Approval
- Encouragement
- To be loved for what he does

</td><td>

She needs:

- Care
- Understanding
- Respect
- To be loved for who she is

</td></tr>
</table>

Emotions

Women tend to be more in touch with their emotions than men are. We express ourselves with more clarity and we give our feelings more room to breath. While men want trust, admiration, approval and encouragement from a relationship, women want respect, understanding, care and reassurance. Crudely translated this means that men want to be loved for what they do and women want to be loved for who they are. They find it easier to play a practical and supportive role – such as doing DIY around the house or being the chief breadwinner or driver – whilst women provide the emotional support, encourage the man in his career and bring up the children.

In this day and age, when women can choose not to have children, are perfectly capable of changing a fuse and have fulfilling and rewarding careers themselves, men are finding that their traditional roles are being increasingly challenged. The truth is, we both need to exercise a little compromise here. Men need to accept that times are changing and women need to understand that it will take more than a generation or two to completely overturn the caveman instinct. While your man can also be your best friend, women will always provide a level of understanding and friendship, which can be hard for a man to match.

How we cope with stress

Men and women cope with stress in differing ways too. In *Men are from Mars, Women are from Venus,* John Gray describes it as men 'going in to their caves'

"Men withdraw, go silent or even disappear when stress gets to them. This shouldn't be seen rejection in a relationship, it's just the way men deal with the shitty stuff of life."

while 'women talk' and there is a certain amount of truth in this. Men withdraw, go silent or even disappear when stress gets to them. This should not be seen as rejection in a relationship, it's just the way men deal with the shitty stuff of life. Women, as ever, talk problems through, analyze them and deal with stressful situations that way. Men often feel like failures under stress, that somehow it's their fault and that they are responsible. They are quick to think that when you are talking to them about your stressful situation that somehow they are to blame and become defensive. Withdrawing into their 'cave' gives them that emotional distance and space that they crave. While we're sharing a bottle of wine with our best mate and talking over problems, men are probably sinking a pint or two on their own in a pub, beating themselves up over something that they may well not be directly responsible for!

The real trouble is that men and women's different ways of coping with stress can cause stress in themselves. We need to take the time to understand the various ways in which the sexes deal with it. Give your man the space and time he needs and don't expect him to talk every problem over with you and resent it when he doesn't. Never take his distance as a sign of rejection.

Chapter 8

flirtmode

the joy of flirting

Brains, wit, intuition?
...you bet!

What is flirting? First and foremost flirting is fun. It is about making people feel good – and that means both the 'flirter' and the 'flirtee'. It makes people smile and feel relaxed and allows people to relate to each other. Most of all, it's all about giving compliments and making someone feel special. It's like having a few drinks. A couple of glasses of your preferred tipple and you feel good, confident, upbeat and playful. Too many and you lose control, become garrulous and loose-tongued and may live to regret what you've said. And it is much the same with flirting. Just indulge in a little, well-applied, well-judged flirting and you'll have a ball. Too much OTT schmoozing and cheesy chat-up lines and you'll both end up feeling embarrassed.

What flirting isn't…Flirting is not leading people on or playing mind games. It doesn't mean that you're after a quick fumble between the sheets any more than you want a committed life-long relationship. You can flirt at work, at a party or even with your friend's dad. It doesn't have to be sexual, aggressive or played out in a dumb or ditsy way. It's not about fluttering your eyelashes and draping yourself all over the nearest male totty. It's not about leaving your intelligence tucked up indoors before you venture out – quite the contrary in fact. Good flirts use their brain, their wit and their intuition.

The joy of flirting

Flirting is a terrific form of communication. To some lucky individuals it comes quite naturally, but in others it has to be learnt. Personal coach Peta Heskell has written an excellent book called *Flirt Coach* which makes it clear just how much fun flirting can be whether you use it in business or in your personal life. Her step-by-step coaching techniques can turn the shyest wallflower into an expert flirt at a level to suit them and where they feel happy and comfortable.

Despite the obvious benefits, flirting has suffered a bad press in recent years – a flirty man can be seen as a sexual-harasser or a letch; a flirty woman as vacuous, flighty and a tease. It's all a question of how you flirt, at what level and with whom. A woman who comes on seriously strong to a married man is employing her flirt tactics badly. A man who delivers a torrent of sexual innuendo, with his eyes firmly fixed on your boobs is not a flirt but a pain in the rear! Both are examples of misjudged flirting levels. Get the levels wrong and you just come over as sad. Get them right and you can have a ball and make someone else feel great too. Learn to gauge the situation, use your instinct and remember that when it comes to flirting, less is more. As we are concerned with dating, this chapter mainly deals with sexual flirting and how to recognize the signals that we give and receive when we fancy someone.

Flirt mode or friend mode?

My friend Johnny is a completely natural flirt. A sensible, attractive man in his late forties, his flirting autopilot kicks in as soon as a remotely sexy woman comes within striking distance. It's as if he can't help himself – oozing charm, wit and flattery from every pore, he was born to flirt. I mentioned this to him one day and said how much I was entertained by the way women seemed to hang on to his every word, holding him with their eyes, while he charmed and flattered with consummate ease. He was shocked, and protested his inno-cence whilst claiming that it was me – not him – who could win a gold medal in the flirting Olympics. And there was me truly believing that I didn't really flirt at all, but was simply friendly, open, warm and curious about people! Johnny and I established that we are clearly both outrageous flirts without really being aware of it.

So…how can we define the difference between a friendly approach and a flirtatious one? It's not always easy to distinguish between the two, especially when you meet someone new. Of course we know when someone is littering their conversation with sexual references and their eyes linger on the parts of your body where their hands would clearly like to follow. Good flirting can be so subtle that it's easy to mistake flirtation as friendliness. For a reserved person, just making polite small talk could be their idea of flirtation, whereas a more confident man, might hold your eyes for a moment, brush your arm and smile sexily. He may of course then go back to talk to his gay partner on the other side of the room, which is as confusing as hell!

Often it's a case of actions speaking louder than words, so you need to take note of a man's body language or what psychologists proudly call 'non-verbal communication'.

There are three instant non-verbal factors that quickly reveal whether someone is flirting, rather than just being friendly. And, as well as using them to spot whether someone is interested in *you*, you can use these techniques yourself when you want to let someone know that you are inter-ested in *them*.

Lingering, direct eye contact

If he looks you directly in the eye for more than a few seconds he's interested. I'm not suggesting that you actually time this, but if you feel a tad uncomfortable, feel the need to avert your gaze to break the moment, or feel the signs of fluttering sexual awakening, he's definitely flirting with you.

He imitates your behaviour

If he tips his head to one side when you do, smiles in direct response to your smile, leans forward when you lean forward or draws on his cigarette or sips his drink when you do, it means he's interested.

He looks at your mouth

The mouth is one of the most sensual parts of the body, being responsible for expressing emotion (as in a smile), the source of the first physical encounter (as in a kiss), and further physical intimacy (as in taste, licking, sucking and so on). You get the picture... If he looks from your eyes to your mouth, lingers there, and then returns his gaze to your eyes, he's definitely flirting and keen. Watch his pupils: if they enlarge, he's finding you sexy...

Grabbing his attention

Okay, so you want to get noticed and flirt with him, but you aren't quite ready to make the first move. Just looking like you're having fun and enjoying yourself is often enough to get you noticed. Sitting with a group of women and hoping to catch someone's eye, while the men sit at the bar nursing their drinks in silence, is not going to lure anyone over! Be careful not to look like you're having *too* good a time though – he might not feel comfortable enough to come over and break up the party.

Once you're relaxed and happy, give him a quick glance, catch his eye and then look away again. Try it again a few moments later, only this time give him a half smile too. That's enough to indicate that you wouldn't be averse to his coming over for a chat. If you're in a situation where you're close enough to hold eye contact, keep it going for a few seconds and smile. It's just about the best signal there is. But do be aware that some men just won't come over. You might just need to go out there and be brave. If he's swapping signals, he may well be interested, just not quite brave enough to

"Make sure you don't look like you're having too good a time, with your girlfriends, though, as he might not feel comfortable enough to come over and break up the party."

come over, especially if you're in a mixed-sex group where he can't be sure – in spite of your signals – that he won't get set upon by your boyfriend!

Being a natural flirt

Why does it seem so easy for some people to flirt? It's generally down to confidence and feeling at ease with yourself. Sometimes it's easy for someone to flirt in a business context, but not in a social one. And vice versa. The expression 'natural' doesn't exclude those who have had to learn to flirt rather than being blessed with flirting skills from an early age, but the following traits are generally found in people with an innate ability to flirt. However, many of these traits can be learnt and will develop as you gain confidence and improve your self-esteem (see Chapter 4: Self-confidence and Self-esteem).

Natural flirts have:

- Good self-esteem
- Belief in themselves
- The flexibility to develop a rapport with many different types of people
- A positive and optimistic attitude to life
- A way of making people feel comfortable in their company
- An ability to ask questions and listen properly to the answers
- Good instincts about what makes other people feel good
- An awareness of their own sexuality and the power of that sexuality
- The ability to pick up on other people's reactions to their flirting
- A sense of when to carry on to the next stage and when to stop flirting
- Fun!

Natural flirts enjoy:

- Meeting people
- New and different social occasions
- Using language to its full advantage
- A shared sense of humour
- Making and managing eye contact
- Giving compliments and making someone else feel good

Daunting isn't it! Aren't they the lucky ones! Still, the rest of us can learn many of these skills and even if we never achieve a black belt in flirting, we can find the level at which we feel comfortable, learn from our mistakes and have a little fun along the way.

Using your voice

Many people are understandably nervous in unfamiliar social situations, and doubly so when the object of their desire is standing right in front of them. It helps to stand tall – that's rich coming from 5ft-nothing me! – but it really does work. I rarely feel intimidated by tall people, partly because I'm seriously addicted to high heels but partly because I stand upright with my shoulders back and my head held high. This also helps me to take control of my voice as it allows me to take deep breaths and, of course, facilitates eye contact.

It is easy to gabble on when you're nervous, but apart from this not being a very good flirting tool, it will also increase the pitch of your voice, which is rarely attractive. Try to talk more slowly, listen properly to his answers and generally take your time. Good flirts don't rush the process – they savour it. Your voice is as important as the words that are spoken. It doesn't really matter whether you have perfect BBC diction or an Essex twang, it's the tone of your voice that really counts. But, if you're really worried about your voice or intonation it might be worth considering a session or two with a voice coach. Try the following exercises – some of them seem a little cranky but they do help:

• Look into a mirror when talking and vary the level of pitch of your voice. Remember, monotonous voices are soporific.

• Imagine you're talking with someone you really fancy. A few 'wow's' and 'that's amazing's' go a long way towards making someone feel good about themselves. It also shows you're interested and varies your intonation.

• Vary the level and pitch of your voice to see what sounds good and feels comfortable. It should be somewhere between a bellow and a whisper.

• Record part of a play, with different characters, into a tape machine, then imagine you're an actor on the radio. Keep trying until you feel relaxed and happy with what you're saying.

• Insert pauses into your conversation for effect – don't make them too long though or you'll appear to have 'dried up'. Make them just long enough to have an effect.

• Lie down, relax and do some deep breathing and then try some of the exercises again.

Learning to flirt

So much of learning to flirt is about developing confidence, the right attitude and above all a belief in yourself. It is not about what you wear, how you wear it or exactly what you say. You can try out your newly-acquired skills one at a time in different social situations. You can't learn to flirt unless you interact with people and actually get out and meet them in a variety of situations. It is not a loner's art. The essence of flirting is to be able to radiate all the best bits of yourself, so that other people want to know more and are attracted to you. Learn to believe that flirting is fun and not a bad thing.

SUCCESSFUL FLIRTING

Accept that not everyone is going to like you and that you will get knockbacks along the way. Hold your head up high and move on.

Five Flirting DOs

❶ First and foremost, you need to learn to like yourself (see Chapter 4: Self-confidence and Self-esteem) so you can learn to accept compliments with grace and without putting yourself down.

❷ Spend less time worrying about your past mistakes and more time thinking about the future. Take a look around and see what is happening now. If your social life is stale, do whatever it takes to improve things by looking for new ways to meet people.

❸ Some of us are born to be worriers, introverts and pessimists. While it's difficult to turn these traits around, it's not impossible if you work at it over time. Try to think of the positive things in your life, not the negative. Be more optimistic. And don't beat yourself up if you make mistakes, however impossibly huge they might seem to be at the time. We all do it and learning to flirt, just like any other skill, takes time and practice to refine.

❹ Smile and pay compliments to people. Tell your work colleague that her new haircut looks great or tell someone how much you appreciate their advice if they've been helpful.

❺ Learn to modulate your voice and vary the tone, speed and pitch when speaking. Cultivate a sexy laugh, but make sure it doesn't sound false: just something you feel comfortable with.

Ten Flirting DON'Ts

These are useful things to remember to do if you want to put off someone that you are *not* interested in, but who is showing interest in you.
Otherwise, try to avoid them!

1 Don't act dumb, or look miserable, bored or snooty.

2 Don't flirt in packs – he may think all his Christmases have come
at once if there's a group of cuties drooling over him, but flirting is
essentially a one-to-one art-form, not a group activity.

3 Don't invade someone's personal space – by all means lean in a
little, but not so that they feel trapped!

4 Don't be sarky or rude – it's not attractive!

5 Don't go over the top when showing and using your body to its
best advantage. A glimpse of cleavage is more enticing than your
D cups running over.

6 Don't stare unblinkingly when maintaining eye contact – he'll
think you've escaped from the local asylum.

7 Don't look over his shoulder when talking to him – he will feel as
if you are searching for your next victim.

8 Don't ignore the signals – if he's not interested, let him go.

9 Don't be too keen, too fast. It's off-putting and seems desperate.

10 Don't drink too much and ruin the whole effect!

Chapter 9

body language

actions speak louder than words

It's that guy again...why <u>does</u> he think I fancy him?!

Body language can speak volumes. We can give away all sorts of things, intentionally or otherwise, just by using seemingly insignificant mannerisms. The way someone walks, stands, uses their hands or their eyes, can give you loud and clear messages, and it helps to know what you are looking for. While flirting makes good use of body language (see Chapter 8: Flirt Mode), this chapter deals solely with non-verbal gestures, posture and expressions known collectively as 'body language'. You'll learn about your own body language and how to put it to good effect plus how to interpret the body language of the guys that you meet.

The way we communicate

Psychologists estimate that up to 93 per cent of social interaction takes place through body language and tone of voice, which means that the actual words we speak make up only 7 per cent! Of this 93 per cent, tone of voice accounts for around 38 per cent leaving a whopping 55 per cent of communication down to body language alone! So a little understanding of the basics of body language would be a valuable tool to have. It enables you to interpret what people are thinking and also helps to reveal what they might be trying to conceal. I'm not suggesting that you turn into a one-woman lie detector but it might be useful to learn to recognize a few signs that will enable you to back off with dignity, or press on with confidence.

You can also enhance your own body language of course. With a little knowledge, you can fine-tune your own non-verbal signals to send guys the kind of message that you want them to receive. It doesn't really matter whether they are experts are not – the truth is that men who have made up their minds about what they want, won't pay much attention to your body language. (Unless you slap 'em hard round the face – then they'll understand!) But men will understand basic, obvious stuff. For example, it's clear that if you gesture openly and widely with both hands when making a particular point, it will have more emphasis and meaning than if you simply use one hand, gently. If you lean in towards them and brush their arm, they should get the message that you're interested. If you lean away from them, arms tightly clasped while looking over their shoulder, they should get that message too!

According to anthropological studies women tend to be more expressive in their body language and are better at reading it in others than men. This may be because traditionally women have had less power than men and it is the role of the less powerful to pay more attention to those with more power. While the power balance may have shifted in the last few decades, we girls have retained our enhanced abilities to interpret body language. In fact, it was once suggested that women should be excluded from jury service in the US because their ability to read body language threatened to interfere with a defendant's right to a fair trial based on the facts alone! But maybe body language is factual evidence too.

"You can fine-tune your own non-verbal signals to send guys the kind of message that you want them to receive."

Many of the gestures and facial expressions that we make are quite unconscious. While we may choose to spend a little time gazing into someone's eyes, we may not be aware that slipping a shoe off or pushing our sleeves up is also an indicator that we fancy someone. But, although we may not be aware that we are making these gestures, once we are aware of them we can play with them to good effect. We can also see when another woman might be interested in the guy that we fancy!

Body language signals work best in 'clusters' i.e. a group of at least three or four signs working together. One or two on their own can be meaningless and will not give a positive enough indication of either interest or disinterest. Also, while men and women do exhibit different body language signs, a great deal of them are common to both sexes. Others, as outlined overleaf, are what psychologists would call 'gender specific messages' and these are only applicable to a specific sex, in part due to the differences in our bodies. While a man might suck in his beer gut to display his pecs, we would suck in our tummies to thrust out our breasts! Similar but different…

Negative body language signs can also be used in clusters. Many of them are defence mechanisms that mean that someone wants the other person to back off. Others may just be the result of nerves or shyness and not significant on their own. Again, look for a group of three or four signs before taking the message on board.

Whether negative or positive, body language works best in harmony with verbal communication. Listening to what someone is saying in association with their body language, is the biggest clue of all as to the level of their sincerity. If he's telling you one thing and and his body language indicates the reverse, then he's probably got something to hide!

Positive body language signs

Look out for these body language signals so you can let someone know that you're interested in them and find out if they are interested in you.

Men and women
- Smiling widely, teeth showing
- Looking around the room, then letting your gaze settle on the 'chosen' one
- Lingering eye contact
- Smoothing clothes or hair
- Running fingers through hair
- Mirroring the other person's body language
- Touching someone
- Leaning in towards or moving closer to the other person
- Head tilting to one side
- Rapid blinking
- Raising/lowering the tone and speed of voice to match the other person
- Undivided attention and focus

Women only
- Pushing back long sleeves to show the softer skin on arms and wrists
- Licking our lips and showing our tongue – but not poking it out!
- Stroking the stem of a wine glass or rubbing a pen.
- Letting a shoe partly slip off our foot and dangling it
- Breasts thrusting forward – obvious I know, but we've all done it!
- Crossing our legs towards a man
- Slowly crossing and uncrossing our legs
- Rubbing a foot against the table leg
- Flicking our hair or twirling it around our fingers
- Hemline creeps up a little to expose more leg
- Our nipples become erect. Yes, I know this happens when it's cold too, but men will see this as a sign of sexual arousal, even if you're in the Arctic!
- Playing with our jewellery, especially stroking a necklace

Men only

- Standing or sitting with legs apart
- Standing with hands on hips
- One or both thumbs tucked into a belt or belt loops, with hands pointing towards their genitals
- Moving into position to block other rivals

Negative body language signs

These body language signals are useful for putting off unwanted suitors – they are also an early warning that he isn't interested so you can make your exit with grace.

Men and women

- Pursed lips
- Fidgeting
- Fiddling with props e.g. making napkin sculptures, picking the labels off beer bottles or shredding beer mats
- Negative grooming gestures – picking fluff off a jumper or pushing nail cuticles back
- Fleeting eye contact
- Looking at the floor
- Small pupils
- Sluggish posture
- Shrugging shoulders
- Hand clenching
- Tightly folded arms
- Leaning or turning away
- Keeping your distance
- Foot tapping or finger drumming
- Fiddling with your collar
- Looking over your shoulder or averting your gaze
- A hand shrug, with palms face up
- No touching, not even 'accidental'

Check him out...

The good news is that men can be pretty obvious when they're interested in you. They may have approached you, in which case it's clear that there's some attraction there, but then what? Are they going to give it a chance or move across the room to the cute chick in the mini skirt whose appeal seems more obvious?

Men give out around four clear signals when they are interested in you, often within the first ten minutes or so. These are:

Providing that they don't have a shaved head, are not bald or wearing a tub of hair gel, they will run their hands through their hair, to draw attention to their crowning glory.

They will suck in their bellies to lose their beer gut and emphasize their upper torso.

They will manoeuvre themselves between you and another person – man or woman – to create a more intimate space, claim their territory and block other potential rivals.

His pupils will dilate – this is not always obvious in a darkened room, especially where they've dilated anyway to accommodate the lack of light, but a definitely a clear signal if you can see it!

Even married or attached men will exhibit these gestures if they fancy their chances. Check out his ring finger before you check out any more of his body language. If the coast looks clear – and it can be difficult to tell in this day and age – let him know that you are interested too with the following easy-to-learn non-verbal body gestures.
  I like to think of them as PETS (Position, Eyes, Touch, Smile).

• **Position:** Turn your body towards him and lean forward slightly, head just tilted to one side.

• **Eyes:** Let your eyes linger on his for a three or four seconds, drop your gaze for a moment and then look into his eyes again for just a second longer.

• **Touch:** Run your fingers through your hair or stroke your face.

• **Smile:** Smile at him, openly and warmly.

That should at least let him know that any further overtures would be welcome, whatever your conversation may be about and if either of you become disinterested as the conversation wears on, then you'll have given nothing away verbally and can feel quite comfortable about moving on. Also, the wonderful thing about PETS is that you can do it in the most unlikely of situations without giving too much away, when talking to a colleague you fancy, for example, or in the supermarket chatting over the deli counter.

First, second or third date body language

So many potential relationships end after just one date. We've all been there and we've all beaten ourselves up afterwards as to why things didn't develop. So how do you recognize whether this date might lead to something more or whether he's likely to move onto pastures new when the evening is over? While a lot of the indicators I've already mentioned come into play, there are some that are more significant than others during the first, second, or third encounter.

If he's interested then he will certainly mirror your movements, gestures and body positions. He will laugh when you laugh. He will lean towards you. He will sit close to you, with his legs or shoulders touching yours. He will keep his eyes on you and give a gentle nod if he likes what you are saying. He may brush your arm or your leg or put his arm behind you on the sofa or chair. He'll look at your lips from time to time, wondering what it would be like to kiss them. He may also look at your other bodily assets as well, thinking the same thing!

If he doesn't seem to do any of these things or constantly looks around the restaurant or bar, then he may be regretting coming out on the date. If he doesn't smile, nod or laugh at your conversation then he may not be smitten. Constant loo visiting can be another sign of boredom – or possibly just a sign of a weak bladder! Men who are disinterested often become vague, defensive or even aggressive. They've got it wrong and they really don't like to fail or waste time. Beware, too, of the man who is suddenly all over you like a rash. He may be thinking that as a relationship, you're not worth pursuing, but as one-night stand, you might be just fine.

First date body language is also critical because this is the time that people are on their best behaviour and so are also out to impress. If there's a wolf in sheep's clothing underneath that smart, polite, attentive exterior then it probably won't begin to show until at least date two (or even date three or four). If he's making a supreme first date effort with his hair, clothes and choice of restaurant, he's probably making a big effort in the body language and flirting stakes too. It may appear that every word that falls from your lips is fascinating and he's nodding and saying all the right stuff in all the right places. Don't be complacent – keep checking him out during each of your subsequent dates with him to see if he changes. In time you're both bound to become more relaxed of course, but certain body language signs never lie. Boredom, disillusionment or disinterest may kick in on date two or three. So watch out for the following giveaway signs:

- He's beginning to fidget and look distracted

- He's fiddling – with his collar, tie, face, the cutlery or his cigarette lighter

- His smile seems more stretched and less spontaneous

- He's not mirroring your body language so much

- He's avoiding eye contact

- He's yawning or rubbing his eyes

Any combination of two or more of these signs and it's not looking good. If this is combined with more stilted conversation or he makes an excuse to leave early as he's got so much work to do tomorrow, it's probably curtains for you. Learn to recognize the signs, react and get in there first and walk away with dignity. If he's keen but he's just tired or stressed, he'll call again.

Your body language style

You need to be careful with your own body language. Too much and you'll come over as a serious space invader, too little and your message won't be received. Imagine you're at a formal do – let's say a wedding reception. You're introduced to someone you think could prove interesting but you are honour-bound to be sociable and so you move on and chat to other people. But you'd like him to know that there's a spark there. Check out the following to see whether you're being too cool and not delivering the right messages, delivering too much, too soon, or just about getting it right.

Too cool...
You smile with your lips closed over your teeth.
You shake his hand limply.
You make conversation but your eyes are darting around the room to check out whether your other mates have arrived yet.
He's telling you how he knows the bride/groom and you react only after he's finished his story.

Your body is slouched, arms crossed.

You have a drink in one hand, a cigarette in the other, so no place for hand gestures.

You'd like to make a little prolonged eye contact, but you need a positive sign from him first.

Time to move on and chat elsewhere – best not say anything more. You don't want to seem needy or desperate.

Too upfront...

You smile with a full, wide grin and give him a wink of the eye.

You give him a bonecrushing and lingering handshake.

You talk animatedly and quickly to make sure that he doesn't have an opportunity for escape just yet.

He's telling you how he knows the bride/groom and you nod constantly, waiting for the moment when you can tell him your story.

Your body is bolt upright, shoulders back, tits out and you take every opportunity to touch his arm.

Lots of big hand gestures, in fact you almost knocked his drink out of his hand at one point!

Your eye contact varies between deep and intense and fluttering your eye-lashes.

Time to move on and chat elsewhere – you say that it was wonderful to meet him, you're so sorry to move on, slip your mobile number into his hand, and say that you'll catch him later on for sure.

Just about right...

You smile with lips open and teeth revealed.

You give him a firm and assured handshake.

You chat, listen and take the opportunity to find out a little more about him. He's telling you how he knows the bride/groom and you listen with interest. You pick up on any coincidental information when you tell him how you know her/him.

Your body is relaxed but straight and you are leaning towards him slightly.

Your hands make a few well-placed gestures.

You scan his whole face, occasionally sharing a few extra seconds of lin-gering eye contact.

Time to move on and chat elsewhere – brush his arm, say it was really nice to meet him and maybe catch him later.

Okay, so these are a slightly exaggerated collection of mannerisms and ges-tures but I've included them in order to make my point. I've been guilty of at least half of the body language crimes in the list above, in an almost identical situation. It is very tempting to get your message over loud and clear in the shortest possible time, but it can be terrifying to men, who think they're being pursued and ensnared. Alternatively, if you don't give off the message that you want them to read, or worse play so cool that you give off negative signals, then that won't get you anywhere either. Being natural and relaxed will help you achieve the body language heaven that you are trying to reach.

Changing your body language

While a lot of body language isn't conscious, there are some skills that can be learned or developed further. Body language reflects your personality and your interest in someone else, so I'm a great believer in changing some of your body language styles to suit your needs. Although it might seem false or odd at first, putting these changes into practice will become easier with time and they'll start to feel much more natural. The other thing to be aware of is that your body language will naturally change in response to another person's reaction to you. If you're both keen and you start to mirror each other's body language, then what started out feeling unnatural, will feel completely natural! Then, hey presto, it all starts to fall into place. Just like flirting, it may seem awkward and uncomfortable at first, but practice – as with any sport or skill – makes perfect…

dating and sex

when is the time right?

For those of you that have turned to this chapter first, I'd better come clean and tell you that it is not about sexual technique, achieving the best orgasm in the world or where to locate the elusive g-spot! There are plenty of good (and a few seriously dire) sex manuals and guides around that can impart that sort of information far better than I can. Some of the ones that I'd recommend are listed on page 163. What this chapter does offer is a little personal advice on the rudiments of sex within early dating: the why's and wherefore's rather than the do's and don'ts. It's about expectations – the importance of sex in a relationship, overcoming some common problems and having a lot of fun, of course! The fact that this chapter is one of the longest in the book is indicative of how important I feel that sex is in any relationship. Get the sex right and a lot of other stuff falls into place naturally. Get it wrong and it can be the undoing of a relationship.

The importance of sex

Sex – and preferably good, satisfying sex – is absolutely key in a relationship. After all, your initial attraction to someone is all about sex – fancying someone, lust, chemistry, call it what you will – so all roads lead back to sex. There are, of course, times when we are too tired or too stressed to make love, or have PMT and would just prefer to snuggle down alone, watch an old movie and eat a huge amount of chocolate. It's absolutely normal. However, regular satisfying sex is instrumental in making a relationship work. Even if the rest of your relationship seems to be just fine, if you are having unsatisfying and/or irregular sex it will eventually get to one of you. The point is that without sex, you just have a friendship. It may be the most awesome, intimate friendship ever but without any sex a friendship is what it will always stay.

Sex is what we have with our lovers – it bonds us together to create a level of intimacy that goes beyond friendship. It's a form of stress release, immense pleasure, costs nothing and uses lots of calories. Research has shown that it both strengthens our immune system and lengthens our lives. Not a bad package of benefits! Added to that, it makes us feel wanted, sexy, confident, cared for and relaxed. That's good sex of course. Bad sex or sex that you have to persuade someone to have against their better judgement makes you frustrated, unattractive, unwanted, tense and dents your self-confidence big time. While this chapter may help maintain or improve an already rewarding sex life, there are more specialist books available that will delve far deeper into ways of helping you to achieve a great sex life than I can here. I really do recommend that you read some of these, even if you think that all is fine and dandy. They're fun, erotic and you're bound to find an angle (or a position!) that you haven't thought of before. No one can have a great sex life all of the time – every relationship has its peaks and troughs – but satisfying and fun sex is just so important that it really is worth ensuring that you nurture it as much as possible.

To tease or not to tease...

Sexual teasing is a little like flirting in that it suffers from some unfortunate misconceptions. Some men interpret teasing as a green light to go the whole hog, when teasing can actually be fun in itself and can be a great prelude in the early days before you have made love with someone. It's a promise of what might just happen at a later date! It's a shame but, all too often, men think that teasing and then not going the whole way is just 'leading them on' or being a 'prick-teaser'. A lot of this is down to the physical build up that men experience sexually, which drives them to need a release when they get past a certain point. They can stop of course – the 'she was asking for it and I couldn't stop' line is just repugnant. The trick of good teasing is either not to get them to this point or to recognize when it happens and ensure that you allow them some physical release, whether it's a hand or a blow job.

One way in which men love to be teased is by watching you pleasuring yourself. It may simply be you stroking or stimulating yourself. Some women feel embarrassed by this, thinking that too much of their body is being exposed and watched, but believe me, he'll only be looking at where your hands are playing! Stockings and suspenders or other erotic clothing will definitely add something to this, as will using a sexual toy of any sort, such as a vibrator. It's provocative, sexy and, above all, fun and exciting for both of you. It's also something that you can do when you're not quite ready for full love making with your new partner. It will definitely have him coming back for more!

Teasing can take many forms: eye contact, body language, flirting, talking about sex and being somewhere where the promise of sex is there, but you just can't get away… yet. Teasing is about build up and anticipation – it's just like prolonged foreplay. It's often recommended by 'sexperts' when men have trouble maintaining an erection or a couple's sex life has deteriorated in some way. A few weeks of teasing and foreplay without actually making love, allows the build up of anticipation that can often kick-start the sexual side of a long-term relationship.

When is the right time to have sex?

I'd love to have the answer to this question as it means I could have personally avoided a whole rash of dating disasters in the last twenty years or so. Too soon and you worry about being seen as a slapper or a tart, in spite of the fact that all you are actually doing is demonstrating the same level of sexual desire as a man. Wait too long and you worry about being seen as frigid or losing the object of your desire to another more willing partner because he thinks that you don't fancy him enough. Basically, you should have sex when it feels right for you i.e. when your instinct guides you in that direction and you feel happy, relaxed, comfortable and horny.

I'm not going to preach or to try and tell you exactly what I think is right or wrong, but I will offer up some advice on which you can base your own judgements. I don't think it's a great idea to leap into bed on the first or even the second or third date. Here's why. If you're looking for something more than casual sex then it's worth holding out for a while – especially if you think this guy could have what it takes to become a serious thing. This is partly because sex is pretty much freely available these days for both sexes. Go into any bar or club, flaunt yourself a little and you will pull, so you can easily just have sex if that's what you really want. So by not having sex straightaway you somehow make it more special. Most guys will definitely try to come on strong to you, as I mentioned before, he's programmed to follow that course, but if he thinks that you might be relationship material then there's a part of him that's also urging you to say 'no' even if his hands, lips and words are all urging you to say yes, right now. If, on the other hand, he's after nothing more than a quick fling or a one-night stand, he'll give up after your refusal and move on to the next person. But remember, he would have moved on anyway if that's the way he was inclined, so at least you've managed to come out of the situation with your dignity intact.

However liberated we think we are – and however many promiscuous phases we've been through – women usually have that nagging doubt that the first date isn't usually the right time for sex. The truth is we need to know a little more about someone before sex feels right. We need to know if we're compatible, whether we've got the same sort of values in life and whether we think we can make each other feel good, even if we're not expecting it to lead to the happy-ever-after. Chemistry and lust are wonderful things but they are dangerous feelings. Holding off for a while won't make them go away, you won't lose those heady feelings. In fact, they'll probably intensify. The more that you get to know him and the nicer he is, the greater the build up of lust and desire and the hotter the sex. You know it makes sense! There are always exceptions to the rule and I know people – as you will too – who hopped into bed on the first date, fell in love and are now together for eternity, without so much as a backwards glance. Of course it happens. But I don't know anyone who wishes that they'd slept with someone earlier than they did, but I know many who wish that they'd waited a bit longer...

Worrying about our bodies...

We all worry about how our bodies look when we're in bed with someone: too fat, too wobbly, too skinny – basically just not the perfect flat stomach, legs up to our armpits and pert breasts that dominate our magazines, newspapers and advertising hoardings. Great sex is all about having confidence, being relaxed, being adventurous, being sexy, having enthusiasm and much more – but it is not about the shape of our bodies or conforming to the 'norm'. It's true that if you feel deeply uncomfortable about your body, you may find it hard to relax and enjoy sex, but being sexy in bed is not about having the body perfect.

For a woman, being good in bed is all about being sexy. Sexy people are not necessarily the most beautiful, the most talented or the most intelligent. A bad hair day or cellulite on your thighs will not stop you being sexy either. It's down to accepting yourself – self-esteem is the key. A new outfit, haircut or a diet all contribute to our feeling good about ourselves and in turn make us feel and act in a sexier way. Only when we feel relatively content in ourselves and comfortable with the person we present to the outside world can we become sexy to others. Sexy people may or may not have the 'perfect' body but what they do is accentuate the positive rather than the negative.

If, in spite of all my reassurances, you're still worried about your body, what can you do? Making love by candlelight is one solution. Soft lighting makes even the flabbiest of bodies beautiful, so light the room with perfumed candles and a few strategically positioned tea-lights. Why not make love by the light of a roaring fire? Push your shoulders out so that your breasts become more pert and your stomach seems flatter if you want to appear slimmer and feel sexier. Or try wearing high-heeled long black leather boots or gorgeous lingerie.

Accentuate your best features. Great legs? Use 'em to their best advantage. Great eyes? Hold his gaze while making love, it's both passionate, exciting and averts his gaze from the bits that you'd rather he didn't dwell on. Great mouth? keep kissing him sensuously. Great bum? Need I go on?

The GIB factor

How do you know if he's got that GIB factor? What is GIB? It's Good In Bed, of course! A number of things will indicate this, but the odds are definitely in your favour if:

He dances well

If he's got rhythm on the dance floor then it's a pretty good bet that he's got rhythm in the sack. It's pretty obvious really – in order to dance well and sexily, he's got to have confidence and be in tune with his body. Two pretty powerful ingredients of inspired sexual performance.

If he's standing with his feet rooted to the floor, while swaying his upper torso in some amorphous, unrelated-to-the-music rhythm or alternatively leaping around like a whirling dervish on speed, he's probably going to be a lacklustre lover. However, make sure that he's also making eye-contact with you and that you're both interacting as you dance. The swaggering, snake-like dance of the arrogant guy (think gold medallion man...) who is only into himself may just turn out to be more selfish than hot in bed.

He has style

He doesn't need to be a male model or spend a fortune on his clothes, but any man who's aware of what he looks good in has that sort of bodily awareness that makes for a good lover. He doesn't need to be a slave to fashion, but he needs to look sexy, well dressed and relaxed. He doesn't need to have bulging biceps or a six-pack, but he does need to give off a sense of style and an awareness of clothes.

Rugby shirts can look cool but football shirts rarely do (unless worn on the field by the likes of Beckham or Owen). Nothing beats a well-cut pair of jeans and a crisp linen shirt or a plain black or white short-sleeved T-shirt. Shirt in or out – depending on the physique.

He's adventurous with food and enjoys dining

It's kind of obvious that a guy who enjoys and savours his food, and is willing to try something new at the dinner table, is also likely to be willing to try something new in bed. It's all down to hedonism. If he seeks and takes pleasure from good food and drink, he's bound to be the same about sex. If his idea of a good meal is shovelling a greasy kebab down on his way back from the pub, he may well just take the same approach in bed – a quick shag to fulfil his needs and he'll roll over and go to sleep...

His touch is generous and electric

Being tactile is critical to the GIB factor. Too little and he'll come over as nervous, hesitant and uncomfortable, which does not generally make for a great sexual experience. Too much, too soon and he'll just seem too eager and intrusive and the whole event might just be over too soon…

If he stands so close to you so your bodies or thighs are almost touching, that's a good sign. If he strokes your hand, lingering over each finger, rather than just holding it limply, that's also good. If your urge is to lean in and move closer, your breathing quickens and you get a stirring in your loins, it's another positive sign.

He's a great kisser

And what about when you get to the first serious kiss? If he kisses you firmly, passionately and manages to caress you elsewhere at the same time, it's time to book that hotel room with the four-poster!

Multi-tasking is not really a male thing but if a man can concentrate on two things at once in bed, then the pleasure zone awaits. The best kiss is passionate and long (though not so long that you begin to wonder if you fed the cat before you came out) and nibbling, licking, soft biting etc. all indicate his potential to deliver sexual variety in bed. Playing aggressive tonsil tennis with you implies a possible lack of foreplay skills…so watch out!

He knows what he wants

A confident man is really sexy in bed. A man who has a clear idea of what gives him pleasure between the sheets is often willing to do the same for you. Men like this usually know what clothes and hairstyle suits them, are fulfilled in their work, flirt well and know how to make you feel good in their company.

Although he may not be the cutest or fittest guy in the room, a confident man will make you feel special in any situation. Coupled with the ability to be both funny and not take himself too seriously, this man's qualities can be a heady combination in the bedroom.

Sexual performance

The more we worry about how 'good' we are, the less likely we are to relax and 'perform' well. These words are inside quotes because performance is so subjective and anyway, you're not there to pass a test! Plus, none of us are great in bed every time, not a single one amongst us. Tiredness, stress or just not really being in the mood all affect our sexual performance. We also worry about being too good – does that mean he might think we've done it too often before? Believe me, enjoyment is what it's all about and if you're a wildcat it in the bedroom and he gets off on that (as he should...) then never beat yourself up about it. You're doing what comes naturally and having fun and there's no earthly, sensible reason why that should be related to the number of sexual partners you've had.

If you are worried about your ability to give and receive sexual pleasure, shedding your inhibitions, having an orgasm every time you make love or any other performance-related anxiety, please look at one or two of the books that I recommend on page 163. They're packed full of sensible and reassuring advice on these topics.

Great sex the first time

As we get to know someone better and become more intimate with them both physically and emotionally, our sex lives should definitely get better. However, first-time sex needn't be a daunting, clumsy process any more than it should be the best time we ever have. There are some great pluses to first-time sex – it's raw, it's new, it zings with sheer lust and can be fantastic – as long as there's a little basic preparation. Without that preparation it can be awkward, over too quickly and frankly disappointing for both partners. Be aware of the following before you sleep with someone for the first time in any new relationship:

Be prepared – Pick the right time and place. Set the mood by turning the lights down low, lighting scented candles and playing a little mood music. Nothing too slushy, but definitely no heavy metal or rock 'n' roll! And make sure you have some condoms to hand – literally. They are one of life's more tedious things but they are a necessity and you don't want to be wondering just which drawer you've left them in at the crucial moment.

Don't unwrap all your presents at once – This is not a competition to see how many different sexual positions you can achieve in one night. You have nothing to prove. Just relax and have fun.

Don't expect fireworks – Sometimes it just takes a little time to find your equilibrium in bed. Just because the chemistry's there, it doesn't ensure that you'll have perfect sex the first time. You may not come and he may be too excited to sustain an erection. You're both nervous – it happens. As long as you talk about it and laugh (not at each other, but *with* each other) one less-than-perfect sex session should not permanently damage your relationship.

Relax and stop worrying – He's not judging your body, well he is a little, but he will gladly overlook most of your so-called 'faults'. And if you really feel that they are that awful – and bodies vary hugely, so they're probably not – then warn him if it makes you feel more relaxed. I have two criss-crossed Caesarean scars, which mark the births of my two wonderful children. I used to feel it necessary to point them out – but it seems that I was the only one who was worried about them. A friend of mine has a third nipple on one of her breasts – she makes light of it by saying that there's an extra one to play with! Certainly a few stretch marks, cellulite dimples or wobbly bits will not put him off. He'll be fretting too – about his love handles, the size of his manhood or coming too soon. Your concerns are nothing compared to his – trust me. There may be a hundred things you know you like in bed but let him try and find out for himself the first time. This is not the moment to tell him you like his fingers stroking your little toe or his tongue in your armpit. Leave it until your second or third sexual encounter to direct him to these things, or he will feel inadequate.

Enjoy – Kiss him slowly, stroke him gently, spend as much time as possible on foreplay and avoid the temptation to go headlong to the main event within the first few minutes. Take your time and enjoy…

Casual sex – no strings attached

The term 'casual sex' implies love-making that is relaxed and laid back, which at its best – and with both parties in the same frame of mind – it can be. The trouble is that the term is also loaded with connotations that you are a 'slut', a 'tart' or a 'slapper' or any of those other phrases than men have coined to describe a women they think is too 'easy'.

All too often being sexually attractive and sexually active can earn a girl a 'reputation' she doesn't want. We should, of course, have moved on from these sexual inequalities by now (which is, after all, what they are) but sadly they still linger on. Even today, it takes a determined sort of ladette, to carry off regular, casual sex with any real belief in herself and without running the risk of being judged by others.

The benefits of casual sex

While casual sex lacks depth and intimacy (the real reason for sex in a meaningful relationship) it certainly has one or two things to recommend it:

• You don't have to worry about what you feel for each other and you can indulge in the physical satisfaction only.

• You can feel totally uninhibited.

• You can carry out a sexual fantasy without worrying about being laughed at or rejected.

• You can choose a partner who excites you sexually but would be unlikely to be compatible as a long-term partner.

• It feels naughty and out of bounds and therefore more exciting.

• It's lust, lust and more lust (what better excuse is there?!).

The potential pitfalls of casual sex

If you're not searching for the perfect mate just yet – you may recently have come out of a long-term relationship and be reluctant to go headlong into another one – but do miss sex, then casual sex may be just right for you. You should be extra specially aware of potential problems though such as:

Feeling guilty or cheap afterwards – if this is how you're feeling, then it may not be the way to go for you.

Always, keep, carry and insist on using condoms, no matter what and no matter who!

Be careful how many people you tell about your affairs – you may feel totally at ease with yourself but others may be quick to judge. If you don't care what they think, then fine.

Beware of married or attached men. They may be perfect for casual sex as they are unlikely to want to move the goalposts of the relationship, but being pursued or harangued by their partner if they find out about you both is not desirable.

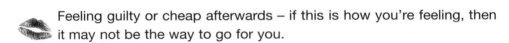

Friends' husbands and boyfriends are *definitely* off limits. It seems obvious, I know, but mistakes can be made…

Keep focused and keep your feelings under control. Sex is such an intimate activity and great sex such a joy, that it can be easy to start falling for someone, originally chosen only as a sexual partner. Don't risk a broken heart – either tell him (you never know, he may be beginning to feel the same way too, but don't bank on it) or get out of the situation while the going is good.

Take extra care and don't take unnecessary risks. Don't go back to his place, until you know him better. Try and make sure that your flatmate's at your place too – at least the first time or, if you live on your own, tell someone about him. Trust your instincts – if there's even a whiff of anything slightly dodgy about him, keep well away.

Help! Our sex drives don't match

Sexual compatibility is definitely important in a relationship, and unless you're willing to compromise by doing it more or less often that you'd like, or being more or less adventurous than really suits you, it could lead to the swift downfall of your new relationship. While some people have naturally high libidos, preferring sex over just about any other activity on offer because they love it 'any time, anywhere, any how'. Others, while enjoying good sex, are just as happy to watch TV and have breakfast in bed or to just have a nice cuddle now and again.

Our sex drives are determined by our genetic makeup, our hormones, our past sexual experiences and how we were brought up to think about sex – whether it's a necessary evil or just doing what comes naturally. And it's pointless beating yourself up about having a lower sex drive than you think is 'normal'. After all, problems in relationships regarding sex are not always the fault of the partner with the lower sex drive any more than they are the fault of the partner with the higher one.

It is also a mistake to think that it's men who always have higher libidos in a relationship – but actually women like sex too, and sometimes more than their partners! Your libido will often change with the seasons – we're definitely hornier in the spring (when the sap is rising!), during the hot summer months, when work is going well, and just before

"It's pointless to beat yourself up about having a lower sex drive than you think is 'normal'."

"If sexual doldrums are prolonged, accompanied by a more general *ennui* or dissatisfaction, or you've simply stopped communicating properly, then there may well be a deeper problem there that needs sorting out."

and often during our period, and when we're feeling content, and so on. It fluctuates according to a number of reasons. Sometimes it's dependent on the partner that we're with. If sex has become predictable and boring, it will inevitably lower our sex drive, just as fantastic, deeply satisfying or loving sex can increase our sex drives.

If your libidos really are poles apart then you may just not be suited to each other. In the early, lustful stages of a relationship then any incompatibility in our libidos is often not noticed. It is only weeks, months or even years down the line that the cracks may begin to show. Sometimes this is down to our unrealistic expectations. We watch TV shows and movies full of sex and read magazine articles about it all the time and it is hard not to believe that everyone except us is having mind-blowing, multi-orgasmic sex on a regular basis. Even with constant injections of variety into our sex lives, new positions, new games and playing with sex toys, even the most loving, long-term relationship can become a bit stale sexually. Or certainly by comparison to what we perceive is happening all around us. This is perfectly natural – almost all relationships go through the sexual doldrums from time to time and it's not necessarily indicative that the end is nigh. If the doldrums are prolonged, accompanied by a more general *ennui* or dissatisfaction, or you've simply stopped communicating properly, then there may well be a deeper problem there that needs sorting out. That said, the biggest libido problems tend to stem from tiredness, stress and hormone imbalances, so check these out before chucking the baby out with the bath water.

While the spirit of compromise or sheer lust can overcome many early libido differences, these are some of the factors that it is useful to have in common to sustain similar sex drives:

 You both like to make love at any time of the day and don't have fixed views on being a morning or an evening person, unless you both agree that you prefer sex at the same time of the day.

 Both partners are equally happy (or reluctant) to communicate their sexual desires, wants, needs and preferences to each other.

You both have similar views on where to have sex i.e. in the bedroom, between the sheets with the lights off, in any room in the house or the sky's the limit – literally, in some cases, like the danger-of-being-found-out mile high club!

You both feel the same way about using sex toys or pleasure aids such as vibrators, massage oil or you wearing stockings, suspenders and killer heels when having sex.

You have a similar attitude towards losing all your inhibitions – it's a disaster when one of you can be a wild cat in bed, while the other is embarrassed about making any noise during sex.

You both have the same attitude towards foreplay or are at least willing to give into the other's needs on a 50/50 basis.

Your sexual health

Is it acceptable for a woman to carry around a condom or two? Does this mean that we're slappers who are up for it and ready for casual sex at the drop of a hat? Or does this mean that we value our lives too much to catch a nasty sexually transmitted disease or something as devastating as AIDS? Let's face it, it's always possible that we might have a little too much to drink and sleep with someone earlier than we would have done if we'd been sober. Isn't it? I think you know the answer to that one. This isn't a crime but it's a crime not to take responsibility for your own health. Don't show your condoms off (hey, nice earrings!) – but keep a couple in your handbag just as you would tampons. Your period won't come on any faster just because you're carrying a tampon any more than you're more likely to leap into bed with the first available candidate just because there's a condom secreted at the bottom of your make-up bag.

> "It's a crime not to take responsibility for your own health. Don't show your condoms off (hey, nice earrings!) – but keep a couple in your handbag just as you would tampons."

It's too easy to think that a man will always have condoms at the ready, just because he's the one who has to wear one. I wouldn't want to play

Russian Roulette with my life, on that assumption, would you? Yes they're ugly, cumbersome and get in the way, but then so are life belts, but it would hardly be the objection when you were drowning, would it now?

CELEBRITY SEX

Here are a few of my favourite quotes on sex, for your amusement:

Woody Allen
Having sex is like playing bridge. If you don't have a good partner, you'd better have a good hand.

Tom Clancy
I believe that sex is one of the most beautiful, natural, wholesome things that money can buy.

Steve Martin
You know that look that women get when they want sex?
No me neither.

George Burns
It isn't premarital sex if you have no intention of getting married.

Lynn Lavner
There are a number of mechanical devices which increase sexual arousal, particularly in women. Chief among these is the Mercedes Benz 380SL.

Chapter 11

mind the
gap

is age difference
an issue?

He's old enough to be my Dad...but he's so much richer!

There are more single women out there than ever before – and what a mixed bag they are. Girls in their teens and early twenties looking for a non-committal, fun relationship; women in their late twenties and early thirties, usually financially independent, looking for a bit more commitment and a longer-term relationship plus some in their mid-thirties or older, whose biological clocks are ticking louder and louder. There are, of course, women from all age groups who are separated, divorced or widowed and looking for some romantic fun.

When searching for a partner, many of us are looking for someone from a similar background with shared interests and who is roughly the same age as us. But it's not always that easy. Sometimes it seems like all the available men are either just out of nappies or about to draw their pensions. But hey, it's not like a ten-year plus age gap matters that much when you get into your twenties or thirties. It's not as if they are a relatively mature twenty and we are still a child of ten or vice versa. Or does it matter? There are pros and cons and it's worth considering some of these, if you're considering dating someone who is significantly older or younger than you.

Let's look at dating an older guy first. It's often very appealing to date someone who earns considerably more money than you and an older man is likely to be better off than a younger one, although not always. You get spoilt, treated like a queen and are able to do things that you only ever dreamt of with this wealthy older man. But this does change the balance of a relation-ship. If you've become used to going 'Dutch' on your dates and enjoy a degree of financial independence within a relationship, this lavish treatment may just become uncomfortable after a time and you might feel that you fear losing that independence or being treated like a 'kept' woman. Sexually an older man may seem daunting – his level of experience seems so much greater, yet he may also seem to tire more easily. He may not want to go out as often as you or enjoy clubbing or going to bars with your mates. It's like-ly that his idea of hanging out on a Sunday afternoon is a round of golf with his friends, rather than a round of drinks with yours.

However, a recent survey has revealed that as women have become more financially independent, with well-paid jobs and careers of their own, the thirty-somethings are moving away from dating the more mature man and onto the younger, more supple and fit toy boys. One in four of us have dated at least one man significantly younger than ourselves and a similar number of women over 40 say that they would like to. With financial independence has come greater confidence and sexual awareness and the fit, toned, glamorous, confident thirty- and forty-something woman has also become increasingly attractive to the younger men. The results of the most recent US Census Bureau also showed that in the year 2000, 12 per cent of all marriages were between older women and younger men.

Toy Boy: older woman/younger man

The basics
Here's to you, Mrs Robinson. This is usually a younger guy looking for some fun in the sack with a more experienced woman. Sometimes all that maturity, confidence and maybe career success will make him really smitten and if it's mutual it can be a fantastic relationship, providing you're not always looking over your shoulder to check out the younger competition, which can be nerve wracking. If you feel that your social life is getting a bit staid, all your mates are settled into couple comfort and you find it hard to meet men of your own age who aren't just looking for little extra-marital fun, dating a younger guy could be just what you need. It puts you back in touch with your younger self, renews your energy levels and can make you feel – and often look – much younger than you are.

Younger guys tend to be less set in their ways and much happier to go with the flow and do more of what you want to do. It's a great opportunity to take the lead, and not just in bed. It's also fantastically good for the ego. I have dated more younger men than older ones. Part of the reason for this is that it is difficult to meet unattached, attractive, bright and funny men in their early forties, but much of it is down to the fact that it is enormous fun. It is also especially rewarding if you relish your independence and are reluctant to get trapped in a 'committed-for-life' relationship just yet.

"Dating a younger guy can give you intimacy and friendship without a feeling that the relationship has to go somewhere."

All the terrific stuff like intimacy, friendship, great sex and feeling good about yourself can be there, without it actually having to 'go' somewhere. But if you're looking for a life partner it may not be ideal, simply because important stages or goals in life, such as the question of having children – or more children – will play a big part in the longer-term scenario. While the issue of children will inevitably have an impact on the durability of a relationship with a younger man, biologically it does actually make good sense. Women live longer than men and reach their sexual peak later, so a 35-year-old woman and a 22-year-old man actually make the ideal biological pairing!

Women of today are fortunate to be in a privileged generation. There is little social stigma left in being single and we singletons can balance work and child-rearing without too many 'tsk-tsks' (especially not from our peers). And there is more advice (and products!) to help us look younger, fitter and sexier than ever before. This liberation often intimidates older men, who are more used to or prefer a different balance, but younger men rarely have these doubts and love the more confident, independent woman who knows what she wants and isn't afraid to go for it. They find it sexy, intriguing, alluring and often more in keeping with their own goals. They respect and expect equality in a relationship whereas the intimidated older man may find it more threatening to his alpha male role. Younger men bring fun back into your life, they'll share basic household chores, encourage you in your career, communicate well and are less afraid to show their emotions.

I have definitely noticed a sea change in a lot my friends. When they were in their teens and twenties, they always went for the older man – or at least one of their own age. These guys had grown up more or less in their generation, listened to the same kind of music, watched the same movies and generally were more likely to be interested in progressing from dating through to a serious relationship, nest building and having a family. Fast forward 10 or 15 years and some of these relationships are still going strong – others have broken up. Those women who now find themselves single again are not willing to spend their social lives as the singletons at couples' dinner parties. They want to be back out there again – in the bars, the clubs and the parties – and they are meeting younger men again – as much by default as by choice. So where do the men of their own age go to socialize?

Clearly in any relationship break up, there should be both a man and a woman back on the dating scene again! My personal view is that men in their late thirties tend to rush headlong into the security of another long-term relationship as fast as they can, while we women pause for breath and use the experience to take stock of our lives and think about what we want out of them. We date for dating's sake and can have a ball. So inevitably, given the above, it often tends to be with the younger man. We are much more able to pick ourselves up, dust ourselves down and start all over again, while men often retreat into what they already know and feel comfortable with.

"Dating a younger man can knock years off your age. Somehow you start to look younger (even though you might feel exhausted!)."

I also believe that dating a younger man can knock years off your age. Somehow you start to look younger (even though you might feel exhausted!). It's something to do with all that adrenaline flowing through your veins as well as the simple feel good factor. An age gap of ten or twelve years or so is perfect – any more and there's a slightly scary possibility that your maternal instincts are driving the relationship! You may also have a problem with the fact that he talks in a language that you don't quite understand and his music sounds much better when it's turned off.

That said, dating a younger man still isn't accepted as the norm. 'Is that her son?', 'She looks old enough to be his mother', and even 'She must be keeping him', are just some of the comments you might have to endure. I say, hold your head up high, feel good about yourself and remind yourself that these women (and they usually are women) are generally motivated by more than a touch of the green-eyed monster…

"We have come a long way in the last decade or so and the Mrs Robinson scenario does not have the same shock factor that it had 30 years ago."

The Press are obsessed with age of course. Joan Collins' 33-year age gap in her current relationship with Percy Gibson is one thing, but to describe the latest Hollywood star's current man as her toy boy because there might be three or four years between them is quite absurd. The trouble is that these comments only serve to reinforce the traditional perception of a 'normal' relationship being a man and woman of more or less the same age or a man who is just a couple of years older. But in spite of this, we have come a long way in the last decade or so and the Mrs Robinson scenario does not have the same shock factor that it had 30 years ago. More and more celebrity women have started to break the age barriers with their partners, including Madonna, Goldie Hawn, Susan Sarandon and Geena Davies.

Sex with a younger man

Sure, all those worries about your body – the wobbly bits, the cellulite or the 'Rubensesque' thighs – are now quadrupled because you are being intimate with a guy whose body could grace the centrefold of Playgirl. But these concerns are more than countered by what you can bring to the bedroom i.e. wisdom, experience and a lack of inhibition. Older women definitely know what they want in bed and what they're doing to their partner. Your body may be less finely honed than that of your younger sister, but you can use those curves to a distinct advantage in bed once you know how. I recommend that you read some of the books listed on page 163 if you want more information on this topic.

Generally speaking the older you are, the more lovers you're likely to have had. And just like anything else in life, the more experience you have, the better you become at it. You've had great sex, lousy sex, sex that you never wanted to stop and sex that had you counting the number of sticky-out bits on the Artex ceiling, whilst willing it to be over quickly. You know what makes you feel good, you're not afraid to ask for it and more importantly, especially for younger men, you know what's likely to make them feel good too.

Younger men adore the sexual confidence that older women have. Older women often take control – a big turn on for the younger man. He's likely to be fitter and more adventurous than an older guy, and will be able to adapt to any position that your imagination and experience dictates. He's not going to fret about how many past lovers you've had either – it's all part of your allure – and you are definitely more likely to give him better oral sex than he's ever had before! You're at your sexual peak and you can enjoy that really slow, sensuous, highly-responsive love-making that men adore and that may be sadly lacking in an encounter with the younger woman.

You are, of course, still more than happy to indulge in an urgent, lust-filled quickie too! Younger women often (wrongly) expect a man to know or discover for himself just what makes her feel good. Older women are generally not afraid to guide a guy's hand to a particular erogenous zone, or just suggest a few games or positions that he may not have already thought of.

The advantages of being with a younger man

- A livelier social life

- His youthful energy and availability

- It takes years off you

- Your sexual experience is a turn-on for him

- Your libidos are in sync

- It's fun and different

- You can be yourself

The disadvantages of being with a younger man

- The disapproval of society

- Being at different stages in your lives and wanting different things

- His music!

- Your energy level!

- Younger men don't often become life-partners

- His friends and family may not accept you so readily

Sugar daddy: younger woman/older man

The basics

Sugar daddy used to be the common term for an older man dating a younger woman. Old-fashioned expression though it is, it was based on the fact that the one sure-fire thing an older man could give to a girl was financial security. These days, as more and more of us have learnt to fend for ourselves financially, it doesn't seem quite so important to bag a wealthy, older guy. It has to be said though, that having someone who is as financially independent as you or more so, does help if you want some luxuries in your life – great holidays, dining out regularly and the promise of a serious trinket or two for Christmas, birthdays, anniversaries or just because. You don't have to worry that he might be after you for your money either. However, not all well-off, older men are necessarily generous with their cash. Many have ex-wives or family to support or are just pathologically mean, but if they are generous, money can definitely make life a whole lot more fun.

Of course not all older men are loaded and dating an older man has plenty of other benefits too. They tend to make better dads, for example, as they have more patience and often more time. They tend to be more chivalrous, sensitive to your needs and are less likely to stray. In fact one friend of mine in his mid-forties who is dating a 22–year-old lives his life in absolute fear that she's going to dump him at any moment.

"Older men tend to make better dads as they have more patience and often more time."

It is also undeniable that if older guys have power or fame that can also be a major attraction. Just look at the affairs of some of our plainer politicians (who shall remain nameless) or the chequered love lives of great rock stars such as Mick Jagger or Rod Stewart! These men are not attractive in the conventional sense, but their aura of experience and power makes them appealing. Psychologists also claim that men are not biologically programmed to fall head-over-heels in love before their fiftieth birthdays. Older men also tend to have acquired confidence, the art of conversation and know what they want out of life. They're much less prone than younger men to play relationship games too. My father, bless him, is 84 years young and when my mother passed away seven years ago, all the local single women, some not much older than me, were racing to bag him! He has money certainly, but more than that he has a zest for life, charisma and a wicked sense of humour!

So what are the down sides to dating these male paragons of virtue? Firstly, they can be much more set in their ways and definitely less interested in clubbing or visiting the latest cool but noisy bar. You might find it more difficult to introduce him into your social circle and he may find it harder to mix with your friends. Your music and movie tastes may be poles apart and he might find it harder to adapt to your tastes than you to his, just because he's a man, and men find it increasingly hard to compromise as they get older.

Sexual attraction can also be a problem. While there are a number of very attractive older men around with seemingly eternal good looks (think Robert Redford, Harrison Ford and Sean Connery), many do suffer from seriously receding hairlines and a propensity to paunch out big time. While we can rely on Lycra, a good fitting bra and carefully applied makeup as props, they have fewer aids at their disposal. However his ageing beauty is often compensated for by his other qualities.

Sex with an older man

Let's start with the positive side of sex with an older man. Just like a woman, he is likely to have had more lovers than the younger guy and therefore chalked up that much more experience. Older men tend to be more sensitive, nurturing and caring in bed – apparently this is due to some of their testosterone turning to oestrogen, basically making them more like women! They take the time to explore your body and will certainly spend longer indulging in foreplay. They don't just want to get your clothes off the minute you are alone. He's also much less likely than a younger man to have any sort of dodgy sexually transmitted diseases. He will often be the sexual leader, teaching you a new trick or two, and taking great care to ensure that you have the pleasure and the orgasm that you deserve.

So much for the good news. The down side to sex with an older man is pretty much as you would imagine... Their bodies aren't so taut and muscular, they lack the agility of the young stud and may have more problems in having or maintaining an erection. They come more quickly first time around and are much slower in standing to attention and being ready to play again, as their recovery period, tends to be longer. They also tend to be less adventurous in bed and may be less willing to try unconventional things, such as mutual masturbation or playing with sex toys. Oral sex may be taboo or at least the giving of it! They're more likely to prefer sex only in the bedroom, with the lights out and in a certain order of events. This makes them generally less sexy and appealing than a younger guy or man of your own age.

"Older men tend to be more sensitive, nurturing and caring in bed – they take the time to explore your body and will certainly spend longer indulging in foreplay."

The advantages of being with an older man

• He may have more money

• Older men make better dads

• They have the attractive allure of power

• They are confident and assured in themselves

• Less game-playing and more honesty

The disadvantage of being with an older man

• Receding hairlines and baldness

• Beer bellies and good-living paunches

• Less socially adept

• More set in their ways

• Children and exes mean he might not be all yours

I have it on good authority (from a friend who's made a study of such things) that if a man is being 'economical' with the truth with regards to his age, you can always check him out by studying the angle of his erect penis! The younger man's penis will stand proud and erect towards his navel. The older he is, the more the angle drops. If it's even showing a hint to pointing downwards, he's definitely old enough to be your dad! Hardly scientific, and I don't suggest taking a protractor to bed to measure him, but it's something fun to look out for...

So we've had a look at the delights and perils of dating a man who is significantly older or younger than you. Both scenarios clearly have their pros and cons.

Do you want him older or younger?

Try this quick quiz for fun to see whether you might be compatible with an older or younger man, or maybe both. There are no 'right' or 'wrong' answers, so just answer honestly.

❶ Are you 28 or older?

❷ Can you accept life's knock backs and move on easily?

❸ Do you adapt to change easily?

❹ Are you a risk taker?

❺ Do you relish new challenges?

6 Do you think of money as 'easy come, easy go'?

7 Are you confident?

8 Do you think of yourself as financially independent?

9 Are you physically fit?

10 Do you think of yourself as emotionally independent?

11 Are many or most of your friends younger than you are are?

12 Do you like to meet new people?

13 Are you relaxed in new social situations?

14 Is your radio tuned to a pop music channel?

15 Do you think it's okay to make the first move?

16 Do strangers guess that you are younger than you really are?

17 Can you imagine a sexual relationship without love?

18 Can you imagine a sexual relationship without friendship?

19 Do you think it's okay for a man to cry?

20 Do you believe anything is possible if you put your mind to it?

21 Have you got varied music tastes?

Answers

More Yes than No answers: then a younger guy might be what you need.
More No than Yes answers: then perhaps the older man is for you.
A balanced mix of Yes and No: then the world is your oyster…

Chapter 12

Relationships

making it work

There are many different types of relationship and in this chapter we'll have a look at the ways in which we meet people and how the environment or situation in which we met that person, can dictate the kind of relationship that it turns out to be.

The office romance

Statistics show that about half of us have had a relationship with a colleague at some time or other and that a further 20 per cent wouldn't rule it out in the future. (Even those of us who wouldn't choose to date a colleague, admit to indulging in some harmless flirting at work from time to time!) We get close to our colleagues and often they become good friends – hardly surprising really when you consider that we often have a great deal in common with them. We have, after all, chosen to work in the same field. And often we spend more time with them than with our own family or partner.

Some companies have made vain attempts to prohibit office relationships, which is a bit like banning office politics or office gossip. While you can choose to turn a blind eye or lay down some ground rules on staff conduct, it just isn't possible to legislate against it completely. It's part of the fabric of working life most of the world over. Most workplace relationships don't cause major corporate disruption if handled with discretion and common sense! However, make sure you know your company policy or views on relationships in the workplace when considering dating someone you work with.

THE PROS OF THE OFFICE ROMANCE

- It can be a slow-burn relationship – from colleague, through friendship to lover – often the nicest way to go.
- There's always someone to have lunch or a drink with after work.
- You've always got loads to talk about and plenty in common.
- You already know a bit about him before you start dating.
- You can share your work journey.
- You've got a date for the office party.
- The 'petty' nuances of work politics won't seem petty to someone who shares the same colleagues.
- You can have great sex in the office after hours!
- You know where he is most of the time, which helps with insecurities.

The office party

In theory this is a terrific place to finally chat up or pull the guy you've fancied for ages or with whom you have been making frantic eye contact over the coffee machine for months. The alcohol is flowing freely, you know everyone there, the atmosphere is great and it's all paid for by the boss. How good does life get...?

However, there are a few important things to remember. Being surrounded by all your colleagues, in whatever state of inebriation they might be, means that while you might think that your flirting and dirty dancing with him is cool and discreet, tongues will be wagging on Monday morning and you'll definitely be the hot topic of conversation. Lots of us have done it, been there and occasionally photocopied our bums too. It's fine if you can handle the gossip afterwards.

> "Even if this is the start of something beautiful, you're still going to be conducting your relationship under the scrutiny of your closest colleagues."

But what happens if the relationship doesn't blossom? He decides that it was great, but for one night only... You can't look him in the eye afterwards and your colleagues are watching your every move and adding considerably to the squirm factor. And, even if this is the start of something beautiful, you're still going to be conducting your relationship under the scrutiny of your closest colleagues and you could end up holding regular Q and A sessions for their entertainment. My view is that while the office party may well be the place to develop a new relationship, it is best to leave the one-night stands well alone.

THE CONS OF THE OFFICE ROMANCE

- Both your careers could suffer if the boss doesn't like it.
- If you're dating the boss, colleagues may see your treatment in the workplace as favouritism and become resentful of you.
- You might fall behind with your work.
- Seeing someone virtually 24/7 can cause friction in a relationship.
- You may have to put up with office gossip and speculation.
- You won't like it if he goes into flirt mode with another colleague – however innocent it might be.
- Ending the relationship is harder and you may have to find a new job.
- If you do end the relationship, you risk bumping into him all the time.
- If he dumps you, your feelings and hurt are there for him to see.

AN OFFICE ROMANCE REALITY CHECK

Discretion is definitely the name of the game here. You don't want to give your boss – or anyone else in a position of influence – any possible excuse, however flimsy, for finding fault with your behaviour in the office as a result of this new relationship.

Check your new beau out
Try to make sure, especially if you're new to the workplace, that he's not the office Lothario and that you aren't just another notch on his desk. Also make sure he's not married or otherwise attached – a definite no-go area.

Keep your concentration
Your mind can wander when you're in a new relationship, and it's all too easy to drift into daydreams about just how gorgeous he was last night. It's even more tempting in the office. There he is looking oh-so-cute in his suit and isn't that a glimpse of the lovebite you gave him still showing on his neck? Don't even think about going there, your behaviour will be noticed.

Keep it out of the office
Lunching or taking the occasional coffee or fag break with him is generally fine, but don't take more breaks than you would normally in a normal day or over a working week.

Don't hang around his desk
Don't make eyes at him by his desk and find every excuse under the sun to pass by him, or play footsie under the boardroom table. A lot of fun can be had by being discreet in the workplace. If you're seeing him later that day in the dating context, being extra discreet in the office and treating him just like a work colleague (which, he is) can build up the anticipation for later on. It's a great tease and you can reap the benefits in just a few hours time...

Watch the email correspondence
Don't lapse into constant emails with the object of your desire. Apart from the fact that it's bound to be noticed if it has an impact on your work output, many companies, like it or not, do check on the flow of email

traffic between colleagues and it could lead to a verbal or written warning. If deemed offensive. If it got out of hand it could also lead to instant dismissal. You have been warned!

Watch his position

And no, that doesn't mean how cute his rear looks when he's bending over the fax machine! The potential perils and pitfalls of office relationships are seriously heightened if your datee is either senior or junior to you. There's always a conflict of interest and office confidentiality to think about if you're either dating the boss or someone who is junior to you, especially if you are also their line manager. Try and date someone on your own level – and preferably in a different department – if you can.

Stop grinning like a woman possessed

Yes, I know you're floating around on cloud nine, but it's both a dead give-away and can be bloody irritating to your other colleagues, who may have left their less-than-perfect love lives at home.

'Fess up'

If the relationship looks like it's going to be long term, reveal your hand. There's no point in trying to keep the relationship under wraps once you're in a remotely settled phase. There is definitely something to be gained from telling just a few close colleagues so that the news spreads around the office. The quickest way to kill off any unpleasant gossip is to be honest.

Don't go into too much detail

Beware of giving too much steamy and intimate info away – even to your closest work mates. If he gets even a whiff of this kind of talk, he'll feel seriously embarrassed (even if you are singing his sexual praises to the hilt) and it may just get you dumped.

No sex in the office

Do not start snogging in the office, fondling each other behind the filing cabinets (or anywhere else you might get caught) or have sex on the bosses desk. (Well… at least not until you're absolutely sure that everyone's gone home, including the office cleaner!)

The Holiday Romance

You've saved hard all year and now you're on holiday with your best mate! Your bikini line is freshly waxed, the weather's gorgeous and the guys on the beach are toned and tanned. How good does life get?

Of course, you may strike lucky and meet a guy who lives pretty close to where you live at home, who's around the same age as you, has similar interests to you and as soon as you're back from your holiday, you can pretty much take up where you left off. But we all know that usually it isn't like that, so I'm going to concentrate on the two-week holiday romance that you might have with someone at the resort, the fellow foreign tourist who lives impossibly far away from your home or the local guy who's staying put when you put your bags on the plane.

Holidays are definitely a time when your defences are down and your libido is up and even if you're happy to be single at home, a little romance when you're away from the stresses and strains of everyday life would be very welcome. My friend Kate and I used to have a code for the men we saw on holiday, which was a useful way of communicating our thoughts without these guys guessing what we were up to. An HA (Hunk Alert) is fairly self-explanatory, an OOH meant Only On Holiday, and finally there was the all too frequent NEOH – Not Even On Holiday.

The sad fact is that the majority of holiday romances rarely turn into anything more lasting, and once the coach has left for the return journey to the airport, it's usually all over. So if you can manage to pack some 'lower expectations than normal' into your holiday baggage along with the suncream and condoms then ultimately you stand less chance of being disappointed. It's bit like meeting new friends on holiday. I've lost count of the number of times that I've swapped contact details with people who I've had huge fun with on holiday and really intended to keep in touch with when I get back home. A phone call, a couple of emails, a Christmas card and then it's almost time to start thinking about the next holiday. I meant to keep in touch, I really wanted to see them again, but life kicked in. My friends, my job and my family became real again after putting normal life on hold for a couple of weeks. And it's the same when it comes to a holiday romance. Even if the intention to keep in touch and see each other again is genuinely there, it takes a really special kind of determination to maintain any kind of meaningful relationship once you are back home.

Holiday Romance Code

- HA – Hunk Alert
- OOH – Only On Holiday
- NEOH – Not Even On Holiday!

The 'L' word

Where you choose to go on holiday will dictate the level of attention that you attract. For example, go to Morocco or Tunisia and you'll find that just about every man pesters you, from the sixteen-year-old hotel bellboy to the toothless old farmer down the road. Greece, Spain or Turkey and the attention levels are still high though not quite so desperate. In France they are a whole lot cooler. All this attention is highly seductive and some of the dishier, younger, more attractive men are really well rehearsed at it, making you feel like the most beautiful creature ever to step off a plane. So unlike the guys at home! And these Adonis's often mean what they say when they are saying it. They'll use the love word within hours of meeting you and really think that they mean it. But it's just not the sort of love that you or I would necessarily relate too. It's the here today, gone tomorrow, out of sight, out of mind kind of love, not the everlasting kind. It's what they do and it's one of the pulling skills that they have developed as the number of attractive foreign girls visiting their country has grown. Even if you are the most prudish compared to some of your mates at home, you will no doubt still be 'easier' than the local girls – the ones that they are sure to end up marrying. Of course, sometimes, against all odds, this kind of romance does work out and results in a happy marriage with 2.4 kids but it is extremely rare…

"The local guys will use the love word within hours of meeting you and really think they mean it."

Hurrah for the fling

Holiday romances are often intense. You see someone every day for a week or two, packing the equivalent of a couple of month's worth of dates into a very small space of time. But it's important to view them primarily as flings. There are few demands on your time, you feel freer than you do when you're working and your pre-holiday diet (plus that golden tan, of course) are all making you feel and look better than you have done for months. It's so easy to fall in love when everything from the beautiful scenery, the cheap drinks and the handsome locals are conspiring to help. For this reason, holiday romances can be very addictive – a holiday just wouldn't be the same without one. And anyway, you don't want to be the only one of your mates who hasn't pulled! It always used to be just the guys who were after the 'quick fling' i.e. the sex-based relation-ship with a little extra garnish on top. Now we girls also want to try it too so we can leave behind our everyday lives and actively seek out a little fun with no intention of pursuing it further once our bags are packed to go home. A fling allows you to be whoever you want to be and then just disappear back into your life back home. So far, so good. Now you know where this is taking us…

COULD IT BE LOVE?

Could it be lurve? Here are five key questions you should ask yourself if you think that it might be...

❶ When you first met him did you think 'Phwoar' or 'this guy is fascinating, I want to know more'?

❷ As the relationship progressed did you think 'this guy is so cute, I'd never have pulled him at home' or 'Wow, I feel like I've known him all my life'?

❸ Was your conversation limited to the basics – 'yes, no, thank you, two pina coladas please', or were you able to have a meaningful language in a mutually understood language?

❹ Did any aspect of his culture shock or surprise you or would you consider integrating into his life and would he integrate well into yours?

❺ Did you just find out his first name or did you discuss his family, education, job, star sign and plans for the future?

Clearly the second of these answers indicates that it is more likely to be something that has a chance of having a longer term outcome, but even then, some of these guys are fantastic at doing and saying all the right things – especially when compared to the often cack-handed and clumsy approach of the boys back home. Many foreign men are weaned on romance and schmoozing as well as looking so much more gorgeous than our pallid home-grown lot, with their golden tans, beach bodies and gorgeous dark eyes...

So, if you are going to have a fling with any of the likely local candidates (and these include the waiters, hotel staff, tour guides and holiday reps, amongst others), then do try and keep it real. See it for what it is; don't expect them to call or write or text after you leave. And keep giving those expectations a regular reality check. And if they do contact you, then that's a pleasant surprise and you can decide whether to gently pursue it. Have fun by all means, but keep your expectations realistic.

THE PROS AND CONS OF
A HOLIDAY ROMANCE

Pros

✓ Higher than average chance of pulling a serious cutie

✓ You can be whoever you want to be and leave your inhibitions at home

✓ Fun in the sun is a better class of fun

✓ (Safe) sex on the beach under the stars

✓ There's a maid to wash those well-used sheets

Cons

✗ Absolutely having to, no-doubts-about-it, use condoms even if you're on the Pill

✗ You've found lurve, your mate hasn't and she's pissed off with playing gooseberry

✗ You might fall harder than you originally intended to

✗ The guys back home suddenly look pale and uninteresting

✗ Sand forever in the parts that you didn't think sand could reach

Holiday sex

Condoms, condoms, condoms. Need I go on…? But I will. This is one seriously non-negotiable area. Holiday sex can lead to Sexually Transmitted Infections (STIs) and pregnancy – neither of which make great mementos of your fabulous holiday or hot fling.

STIs

You will, no doubt, go for someone with adequate personal hygiene, but while cleanliness may be next to godliness, it is no protection against AIDS, gonorrhoea, syphilis, genital warts, chlamydia, pelvic inflammatory disease, trichomoniasis and a whole host of other sexually transmitted infections with equally terrifying names and pretty horrible consequences. And even condoms won't protect you from the unpleasantness of pubic lice or scabies. So while those delicious and cheap cocktails might have loosened your tongue, think really hard before they loosen your knicker elastic too. If you do come home with any unusual symptoms, such as vaginal discharge or pain on peeing or intercourse, you must go and see your doctor or local STI clinic as soon as possible. Most infections need to be cleared up with a course or two of antibiotics – they will not go away by themselves.

Pregnancy
If you're on the Pill, make sure you stick to your routine of taking it at the same time of day. If you're sick or have a tummy upset, you could get pregnant, so as well as needing to use condoms as protection against STIs you'll need them to protect you from an unwanted pregnancy as well.

Long-distance relationships

So, the holiday romance has blossomed into something more. Or perhaps the guy you've been seeing for a few months has gone off to university or taken up an 'opportunity of a lifetime' job that's taking him hundreds of miles away. You've been used to seeing each other at least twice a week for months now, he's the best thing since sliced bread and now he's changing all the rules. How are you going to cope? Keeping a relationship going when he lived on the other side of town was bad enough, but when he's overseas or at the end of a seemingly endless train journey, it can be tougher still. Undoubtedly some of the newer technological innovations such as mobile phones, email and text messages help enormously. No more mugging the postman for that long-awaited letter or staying in night after night waiting for his call to the landline. But still, all the webcams and video phones in the world can't compensate for actually being with someone. Travelling to see someone some distance away can be expensive and when you do see each other it can be awkward because you know you've got to pack as much fun into this weekend as possible, and that can be a heavy burden to carry.

That said, long-distance relationships can also be magical, romantic, passionate – and unreal. To make them succeed, you need to turn the negative into the positive. On the plus side, you can remain independent, still go out with your girlfriends, indulge yourself with your own space, join a gym, watch a girlie video – do all the stuff singles still do and enjoy, yet you've still got a loving relationship at the end of the day. Travelling by plane is quicker, easier, and cheaper than ever now – often cheaper than train travel and certainly faster. You can make every holiday or weekend really special by planning ahead so that there's plenty of time to go out and play as well as time in bed. Sending sexy late night text messages is possible from virtually anywhere in the world. As is telephone sex! It isn't easy though.

The downside to long-distance relationships – apart from the cost of travel and the lack of sex – is the fact that there can be jealousy, loneliness and a lack of continuity in your intimacy. The most important thing is for you both to actually believe that this relationship will work in due course. That one day you will be back together again and living in the same place – either when his course has finished or when you find a job near him. If there isn't a reward, compromise on both sides and a common goal it's all going to seem fairly fruitless after a while. Keep the little bits of gossip going, don't think you can only talk about major events and keep up regular emailing, calls, texts – whatever works for you. You need to be able to trust him, miss him, keep the lines of communication open, but get on with your own life at the same time. It's never easy, but definitely possible…

Inappropriate Relationships

So what makes a relationship inappropriate? After all, isn't one woman's meat another woman's poison? I don't want to get in the issues relating to dating someone of a different colour, religion or culture to your own, here. Most relationships that fall into this category come with their own, inherent problems (but, hey, which relationships don't?). Let's look instead at some of the obvious levels of inappropriateness that are probably common to us all.

Dating married or otherwise attached men (unless you can be sure that they are living apart from their wife or partner) is a definite no go area. Plenty of us have heard the phrases 'my wife doesn't understand me' and 'as soon as I can sort things out, I'll leave her' but the truth is if that if his relationship's at that sort of point, shouldn't he do the decent thing, sort it out and leave before moving on to another one? A lot of men use the start of a new relationship as a catalyst to end an existing one, but it's always better to make a clean break before embarking on a new relationship, otherwise it's just stressful and unnecessarily complicated from the start. And if children are involved as well, it's complicated in spades.

Apart from this major 'no-fly zone', there's a whole world of other inappropriate relationships as well, each with its own unique pitfalls to look out for.

"Dating married or otherwise attached men (unless you're sure they are separated and living apart from their wife or partner) is a definite no go area."

Dating bad boys

They're sexy, exciting, convention-defying and usually look like they'd be seriously hot in bed, which they often are. And they allow you to let your hair down (sexually speaking) in a way in which you think other people might judge as 'bad'. The rough 'n' ready bad boy who doesn't give a monkey's will always have the earthy appeal that their more conventional brothers don't

"Bad boys are often passionate and unorthodox in bed so there's always a surprise in store."

have. They are forbidden fruit and all the more delicious for it. Eating chocolate truffles in bed at 3am, drinking too many tequila slammers with the girls, smoking a spliff for the first time – all definitely naughty but way too much fun to forego, relinquish or regret not ever having done.

Dating a bad boy is definitely an adventure. They're very often passionate and unorthodox in bed so there's always a surprise in store. There is also an undeniable element of rebellion in dating a bad boy – your parents, even your friends – may well not approve and that's a major part of the excitement. A guy who is mad, bad and dangerous to know appeals to the risk-taker in us. Interestingly, we often turn to men like this when we've just come out of a relationship that had become dull and predictable.

If you keep your eye on the ball – and don't expect too much from this relationship – it can be a wonderful, exhilirating thing. Bad boys may have their tender moments – which just adds to the excitement of it all – but they are unlikely to want to be chained to you for the long-term. And if they do, it may be because you offer the emotional security they have lacked in the past. You may end up being the giver, the carer and becoming more of a mother figure to him than a lover.

A few tips when dating that bad boy

Don't get taken for a ride
Bad boys can be irresponsible and carefree not only with their own possessions but with other people's as well – including yours – so be careful when lending him money, your car or your flat. He needs to learn to take responsibility for himself. You are not his keeper.

Keep the messing about in the bedroom
If he's really beginning to take over your life and causing problems with your job, your friends or your family and shows no sign of compromise or guilt, get out fast, before he sucks you into a downward spiral with him. It just isn't worth it.

Take regular reality checks on your feelings

He's unlikely to become perfect relationship material (although it's not entirely unheard of). While you should encourage him to express his feelings and open up – which may be a first for him – bad boys are often extraordinarily charming and emotionally manipulative. Don't fall in love without being prepared to face the consequences.

Don't get addicted to him

Dating bad boys can be very exciting, so much so that you may just want to keep coming back for more. This addiction to bad boys often stems from your upbringing. If your parents treated you harshly or found it difficult to show you love, you may try to seek out someone who makes you feel the same way in your adult relationships. Sometimes, though, its quite the opposite: you've had parents who adored and emotionally cosseted you, making it difficult for you to grow up in your own way. Now you're doing – and enjoying – the kind of rebellion most of us went through in our adolescence. It's not an easy cycle to understand or break out of, but it is necessary if you're finally going to secure yourself a loving, fulfilling relationship.

Second time around – taking him back

It's all over. You've gone through the hurt and the anger, bored everyone who'll give you the time of day, binned the tissue mountain you created, destroyed all your photos of him and now you're finally getting your life back on track. Sure, you still miss him – and how! – but you can cope. And then he calls you. He's made this awful mistake. He's in bits without you, and it's taken time apart to realize just how important you are to him.

Gulp. What now?

All the sensible bits of you are firmly saying 'No, not again', but then a huge uncontrollable surge of the Meg Ryan-like 'Yes, yes, yes' kicks in and over-rides that sensible you in an instant. There is a god! And so you make a date. And it's bliss. All the past problems have just disappeared. You knew it was right. Wrong!

The truth is that you're probably just papering over the cracks. The same cracks that will emerge once the second honeymoon period is over. I say 'probably' because there are some cases where what he has said is all genuine and the relationship will work out. It depends on what made you break up in the first place. If he treated you badly, he will again. If he can't wait to make love to you again, he's probably just missing regular sex. The girl he left you for has just dumped him and he wants a bit of comfort. Harsh stuff, but it's so often true. It might work out second time around but you'd be wise to know what you want from him from the outset and stick to your guns. Do you want to cry that river again? Do you buffalo...

Dating your friend's ex

Dating a pal's man behind her back is an accident waiting to happen. If your eyes lock and there's chemistry between you like never before, let him do the decent thing. Break it off with her, give yourselves a decent interval of a few weeks and then see what happens. The odds are high that you'll lose that friend, come what may, as it's a bitter pill for her to swallow. So be warned and make your choice carefully. Close girlfriends are hard to come by. And remember that if he can be that fickle and disloyal while dating your close mate, he may be prone to that common dating disease 'wandering eye syndrome' – next time it could be you that he leaves for one of your friends...

"The odds are high that you'll lose that friend if you date her ex come what may, as it's a bitter pill for her to swallow."

Dating a friend's ex is much more acceptable after a few weeks or months have passed since the end of their relationship. Wounds will have had time to heal – on both sides – and you're much more likely to keep your original friendship with your girlfriend. She may even still agree to be the bridesmaid at your wedding! If she is a close friend, make sure you tell her before things get serious. Turning up at her birthday party with her ex on your arm, isn't the best way to let her know, either.

Dating on the rebound

You miss him badly. You broke up weeks ago, yet you still miss the warmth, intimacy, companionship and sex. Your heart leaps every time you get a text message alert and sinks again when it turns out to be your best friend. What could be simpler than replacing him with another version – it worked when you were little and the goldfish you won at the funfair died... You simply went out and bought another one that looked pretty much the same.

I've already said that I believe that sometimes finding a new relationship is the perfect way of getting over the loss and pain of the last. It can be a time full of hope and anticipation and it can be the ideal antidote to that slightly 'empty-to-the-pit-of-your-stomach' feeling that you get when a relationship is over, regardless of who did the ditching. That said, it is important to let the old wounds heal and learn something from past loves in order to move on. Some of us *can* do this while dating someone else; others need a little more time alone before embarking on a new relationship. It partly depends on what kind of person you are, as well as the seriousness of your last relationship. If it was not terribly significant and it's fun you're after, just go for it.

But if you thought that the last man might have been 'the one' and you can hardly bear to turn the radio on in case you hear 'your' song and you'll start crying again, then you really should allow yourself the space and time you need to recover properly. After all, it's one thing to replace a dead goldfish and quite another to replace your dog after he's been part of your family for fifteen years…

The other thing to bear in mind when you've recently come out of a meaningful relationship is that we all tend to exercise a serious lack of judgement in choosing our next partner. We're so busy falling over ourselves to replace our lost love, with a shinier, newer, less damaged relationship, that even the geeky-looking guy in the corner of the bar who throws us a glance and a friendly smile can be strangely appealing. Poor judgement aside, it's important to take any rebound relationship slowly.

Things to avoid when dating on the rebound

Don't try and hurry things along in order to achieve the same loving nirvana you had with 'him' after five years – it may scare the new datee off and it won't allow you the time or clarity of vision to actually see whether that's where the relationship should or shouldn't be heading.

Don't be tempted to compare and contrast your current guy to the last one – it might take a monumental effort, but this time you've just got to go with the flow.

Bad Relationships

What exactly *is* a bad relationship? After all, going out with a boring man or one who doesn't wash properly is not good. But a bad relationship is something more – it's one that's damaging in some way.

Clearly, a relationship in which you are abused by your partner – either emotionally or physically – is very bad indeed and you must take drastic and immediate action to end it. But there are other more subtle signs of a bad relationship, which will often be as obvious as hell to your closest friends, while you may be totally unaware of any problem. Worse still, if you're really serious about this man, you probably won't take kindly to having this pointed out either. I used to go out with a guy who I thought was great. As a

"The signs of a bad relationship, which will often be as obvious as hell to your closest friends, may leave you totally unaware of any problem."

reasonably bright and confident sort of person, I thought he was smart and clever. I liked the fact that he never let me get away with being too domineering in company, which I had a tendency to do at the time. However, my closest friends, who loved me as I was, just thought he was a control freak who constantly undermined me. They couldn't understand what on earth I saw in him. In the end, they were right, it *was* a bad relationship. In due course he undermined my confidence and it took a while for me to bounce back.

There are plenty of signs to look out for to check that you're not in a bad relationship (see the list below). Otherwise, ask your best and most honest friends for their feedback. Even if you don't agree with them at the time, it may help you look at your new relationship in an objective way and that could help you avoid a lot of heartache and trouble later on down the line.

Signs of a Bad Relationship

So what are signs that you might be in a bad relationship? Have a little look at this lot and see if any of them ring any bells!

• He seems moody and jealous of your friends and past relationships.

• You might not actually argue, but there's definitely a lot of niggling and one-upmanship going on.

• He seems to veer between being devoted to you one minute and all but ignoring you the next.

• He's always vague about the next time you'll see him.

• He criticizes or undermines you, especially in public.

• He has unpredictable mood swings.

• He borrows money and doesn't ever pay you back.

• Your most trusted friends can't understand what you see in him.

• In a relationship based on give and take, you have a sneaking suspicion that you may be doing most of the giving, while he seems to be doing all the taking.

• The sex is great, but otherwise your compatibility is pretty non-existent.

Flings

Whilst it can be an indication that you are in a bad relationship, having great sex but little else in common can also be a good premise on which to base having a fling! A lust-filled, sex-based, short-lived romp with a gorgeous, sexy hunk whose brawn definitely outstrips his brain can be huge fun. So what that it's meaningless and there's no way on god's earth that it's going to lead to

> "Having flings gives you an amazing license to practice your flirting and sexual skills."

happy-ever-after? You know that already and that's the whole point. It only becomes a problem if you're not honest about your motives with the other person or if you become so addicted to flings that you can't see yourself in any other sort of relationship – not because your friends can't see the point or think that you're 'wasting your time'.

There are times in all our lives when we're just not ready for a serious or even a meaningful relationship. Perhaps you've just come out of a long-term relationship. Maybe that gorgeous cutie at work is only around for three months and he's just too good an opportunity to miss. Having flings gives you an amazing license to practice your flirting and sexual skills. Providing neither of you is in another relationship already and you practice safe sex, who's going to get hurt? It's great for your self-esteem and allows you to release your inhibitions. And all that sex will burn up those calories in a way that any kind of gym equipment – however high-tech – would find it very hard to compete with! You do need to embark on a fling with your head straight though. And make sure you keep reminding yourself that a fling is *all* it is or you could be setting yourself up for a fall.

While there are many great reasons to have a fling, there are also times in our lives when having a fling is not such a fab idea, or when our motives might not be the best.

Go ahead and have a ball if:

- You're both unattached.

- You're not ready for anything more serious – for whatever reason.

- You can be honest with your partner about your motives.

- You're still shopping around for the sort of guy that might suit a more long-term relationship further down the line.

- Life as a singleton is just what you need right now, but hell, you miss sex!

Think before you go there if:

- One or both of you is in a relationship.

- You're lonely and looking for companionship.

- You truly hope that it will turn into something else in due course.

- You don't really approve but everybody else seems to be doing it.

- You actually want a 'proper' relationship but they all seem to end up as flings so it's better than nothing.

Matched and dispatched – how to end it

I've left the hard bit right 'til the end…

The relationship just isn't doing it for you any more, you've weathered the bad bits, but you've realized that you'd be happier without him than with him, even if there are still some good bits. Unless he's behaved like a complete bastard throughout, it's always tough to end a relationship. But almost all of us, at some time in our lives, are faced with the stomach-churning decision of breaking up with someone that we may still care about deeply. The temptation to postpone the moment to a later date can be overwhelming, especially if you think your partner has no inkling of what's to come. The guilt is horrendous and just the thought of uttering those devastating words 'I'm sorry, but it's over' fills you with dread. So what can you do to ease the pain for him and how do you overcome those feelings of guilt and face the decision head on?

Doing the right thing

Sometimes it helps to think of it in terms of 'doing the right thing' – you may actually be doing your partner a favour (though never say that to them, they might agree further down the line, but generally not when the bombshell is being dropped). They may think that the relationship is in great shape, which it clearly isn't, they just haven't realized it yet.

Very early on in a relationship – say in the first month or two – the 'I'll just ignore his calls and texts until he gets the message' approach, which is cowardly but understandable (and we've all done it…) might just work. However, any relationship with any depth, however brief, deserves the personal touch. It really should be finished face to face – tough as hell for you, but much fairer to him and more dignified for both of you. A slightly obvious point, but worth mentioning all the same – do always say what you have to say at the start of an evening… never leave it until after dessert.

It's very tempting to send an email or worse still, a text, when ending a relationship, but it is, frankly, a shitty thing to do. Keep reminding yourself how you'd feel if you opened up your emails in the office one morning, and there among the request from the boss for a meeting and the general spam offering you cheaper car or health insurance nestled an email from 'him' telling you that you've been dumped, however silver-tongued he is about it. Phoning is a no-no too, unless you're still only a few dates in. It's not only cold, but impersonal and cowardly too.

It's got to be face to face and it will go much better if you can prepare the way a little beforehand. Not so much that he goes into a blind panic and spends the intervening hours wondering just which terminal illness you have, but just something along the lines of 'we need to talk'. A public place is good, but make sure you choose somewhere discreet and quietish rather than a trendy bar on a Friday night where you have to shout to be heard. Don't choose your mutually favourite place either. It's important that he retains some dignity out of all this – keep reminding yourself of how you'd feel and how you'd 'like' to be dumped.

Make a clean break

There's no nice way to bring the guillotine down on a relationship, but some ways are nicer than others. However, do beware of being too nice. I once ended it with someone, by telling him that he was a great guy – kind, generous, funny, terrific in bed and so on. He reacted by asking me why I was ending it if he was so great. I have to say that convinced though I was that we had no future and we were better off apart, I did such a 'nice' job of ending it, that even I was momentarily confused! Whatever the actual words you use, he should be left in no doubt that it is over.

We all need closure at the end of a relationship – it helps us move on. You will feel guilty, wretched and really mean, but a clean break is what's required. There's no need to be cruel, but you must be firm. Something along the lines of 'I still care about you, but I don't fancy you any more' or

"When you come to the end of the road, a clean break is what's needed. There's no need to be cruel, but you must be firm."

'I'm not getting what I need out of this relationship' is fine. Talk it through for a while – he's bound to have something to say about it, he may fall to pieces, get angry, or try to convince you that you're doing the wrong thing. He may, on the other hand agree that you are right and feel relieved that he wasn't the one who had to pluck up the courage to break it off. Your instinct and the recent events of your individual relationship will help you anticipate the outcome. Conversely, you may feel like the bitch from hell, but don't let him persuade you to change your mind, if you are resolute that it has to end. Make him feel as good as you can – tell him that he's a great guy for someone, but not for you.

A lot of guys react to being dumped, by just walking out. They find it hard to face up to the sudden rush of emotion and shock – even if they were half expecting it – and need to get out as soon as possible so they can lick their wounds in private. If he has walked out – or just said little before leaving – don't panic and start phoning him to see how he is or where he's gone. He's much more likely to be getting off his trolley in a nearby bar than throwing himself off the nearest tall building. However, texting him the next day (thank god for mobile phones) to see how he is would be a nice gesture. He may not want to reply, but at least you've made the move. Sending another text a few days later is good too – or maybe a call to one of his close mates to see how he is. Then leave it, he may not want to talk about it, especially not with you. That's life.

Staying friends

What next? He may not have been the one for you but he was a great guy and you do want to keep him as a mate. Give him time and space to get over his hurt and restore his wounded pride and dignity. Call him after a few months and maybe suggest that you go out for a drink, but be very careful that you are not giving him false hopes that you could get back together again. You need to leave it months rather than weeks, otherwise false hope could set in and that seemingly harmless 'let's meet for a beer' could really set him back emotionally. And remember that if you do become mates, it's bound to be a different sort of relationship. It will be much less intimate now, so you need to tread carefully to check the lie of the land. He isn't a girlfriend and he will not take kindly to hearing about the finer details of your sex life with his successor!

Chapter 13

Love@ First Site

techno-dating

We live, and date, in a fantastic age. While previous generations only had the traditional meeting places – parties, dances, through friends and so on – we now have access to lots of less conventional ways of hooking up with people. Some of these exist because of advances in technology and some are the result of a creative person thinking of ways to tap into the huge potential of the ever-increasing singles market. We can also take advantage of relatively new ways of communicating, such as mobile phones, text messaging and email, and these have radically altered the rules of dating over the last few years. So is it worth giving these new ways a try? It really depends on what takes your fancy. While computer-dating and texting may not be on the brink of taking over the world of dating completely, they are useful methods of meeting and keeping in contact with people and a great 'add on' to the more conventional methods. And anything we can do to widen our options is worth considering!

Love@First Site – Internet Dating

The basics

Apparently, there are several million of us out there looking for love on the World Wide Web at any one time. But websites can vary enormously – some are little more than 'meet markets' asking for the most basic details like your age, job and location. Others go into much more depth, taking into account details such as your education, your favourite social activities – even your attitude to housework and the magazines that you read! The more detailed the information requested, the more likely you are to enable a microchip to match you up. Many of the internet dating sites are international so unless you want to be contacted by people from all over the world it's better to restrict your search to people living relatively close to you.

For a smallish sum each month, you can tap into tens of thousands of possible partners. It is always better to post a photo on the site as this will result in a higher number of approaches or replies as well as making your virtual self seem more real. There are some seriously good looking men out there (as well as some very sad cases indeed) but be warned, not all are what they seem. Some men post photos of themselves that are at least ten years out of date or worse, simply not them at all. I've seen Pierce Brosnan and a hunky male model from a catalogue on one site! And if they don't have a photo? Rather than hiding their light under a bushel, they're likely to be either horrendously ugly or married and therefore living in fear of being recognized.

As with any other kind of dating, it's best to be honest from the outset. Your age, job, smoking and drinking habits, music tastes, sport and social interests and so on that you give, should accurately reflect the real you. The only proviso here is that you should adopt a 'cyber handle' that isn't your real name, to avoid any problems with the handful of nutters out there. Try and think of a fun name. MsPerfectnot or Sassychick is preferable to Jane123 or Nicegirlseeksbloke. Also, as well as making your profile as honest as possible, make it as much fun and as appealing as you can. There's a lot of cyber competition out there!

Once you are ready to go you can check out the photos of literally thousands of men, depending on how broad your categories and preferences are – such as age, location, level of education, looks and so on. You can be proactive and mail them through the site when they're offline, or message them (often called whispering) when they're online. It's like an email chat. Or you can just wait for them to get in touch with you. If the messages are offensive in any way – and some have to be seen to be believed – many sites will allow you to block people so that they can't get back in touch with you again without the offender knowing what has happened.

You are under no obligation to answer any of your messages of course, but if they're inoffensive enough, it's polite to reply even if they don't float your boat. Though sometimes even a knockback is enough to encourage further contact from some thick-skinned men. When you've taken a little time to find out about them and establish whether or not you share any common ground you could arrange to chat to them on the phone with a view to setting up a date. This is always a good idea as his voice and phone manner will tell you a lot about him. Some guys, while happy to chat nineteen to the dozen online, balk at actually meeting you. Presumably they either have something to hide – such as a wife and four kids – or they are not what they purport to be. They can also be just computer nerds who get off on having a virtual conversation.

People often wonder how safe internet dating is. My view is that there are certainly crazy guys out there – maybe even the odd mass murderer or rapist – but if you choose your website with care, exercise basic safety precautions and use your instincts wisely, it's no more dangerous – and possibly even less so – than meeting a stranger in a bar or a club.

Safe cyberdating

@ Don't choose a sexually provocative handle, otherwise you'll get a flood of dirty messages. So avoid MissWhiplash, Sexkitten or Givesgoodhead.

@ Be wary of the handles that men give themselves – Pussylicker or Bondagemerchant are unlikely to want a first date in Starbucks.

@ Be very cautious about giving away your mobile phone number – wait until your instincts tell you that it's right.

@ Take it slowly, don't go on a face-to-face date after just a few 'whispers'.

@ Don't accept everything you read, use your instincts and judgement.

@ Block or report the offensive jerks – most websites dump 'em after a number of bad reports.

@ Setting up a hotmail account, or similar, without using your real name, is a good idea when giving out your email address.

@ Don't give a guy your business address unless you really feel you can trust him – you don't want him stalking your office.

@ If you have his full name, check him out prior to the date. Type his name into a good search engine such as Google or check Friends Reunited.

@ Arrange to meet in a public place, like a bar, pub or coffee shop.

@ If you feel at all uncomfortable, threatened or compromised, excuse yourself and leave.

@ Always let a girlfriend know where you are and ask her to ring your mobile an hour or so into the date.

@ Don't get into his car unless you feel ultra safe.

@ Don't ask him back to your place on the first date.

@ And definitely don't go back to his!

@ Don't even think about falling in virtual lurve – you *must* meet them first.

The 21st-century dating agency

The basics

Dating agencies have come a long way since it was just a simple matter of filling out a questionnaire, sending it off and lo, a mixed bag of male profiles was delivered to your door. They are now operating in a much more competitive world and have had to spruce up their act. Dating agencies – or introduction agencies – as they now prefer to be called, tend to be for the more 'mature' client (30+) and have diversified into intimate dinner parties and even lunch dates, for busy office workers who find it hard to get away for an evening. They are not a cheap option, but rather than let a microchip choose your ideal guy, an experienced member of staff will analyze your profile and find you a suitable match. They also vet their clients, so you're far less likely to end up with a weirdo than if you use the internet dating method. Some agencies also have dedicated websites of their own. Here are the pros and cons of agency dating:

Pros

✓ Access to men who have been hand-picked for you by a human being.

✓ You can be as specific as you like about the kind of guy you'd like to meet.

✓ The men you meet tend to have money as it's not a cheap option.

✓ They also tend to be serious about having a meaningful relationship, rather than just looking for sex.

Cons

✗ Even the most skilled staff member can't legislate for chemistry – the stomach churning hots that you get when you see someone you think is gorgeous.

✗ There's no hiding your light under a bushel here – you have to be serious and focused about finding a mate.

✗ It's expensive and not guaranteed.

✗ It's somehow more calculated and clinical than other ways of meeting a guy – and not as suitable for more independent types who like to do the choosing.

PROS AND CONS OF CYBERDATING

Internet dating is definitely losing its stigma and becoming an acceptable way to meet people – just mention it to a group of people and watch the other internet datees come out of the closet! Where else could you find such a wide and varied selection of single men all looking for a date?

There are some irritating and frequently repeated cyberdating acronyms that it's worth knowing about: LOL (laugh out loud), LMAO (laughing my arse off) and TIC (tongue in cheek).

Pros

It's a great hunting ground for busy, single professionals, especially if you work in a female dominated industry and find it hard to meet men.

You can log on whenever it suits you – after work, a night out or over breakfast. There will always be people to chat to online.

You can go on a virtual date and flirt to your heart's content, while wearing no make-up and your oldest underwear.

You can often find out more about someone before dating them than you could from a bar or club pick up.

Even if your dating doesn't work out, you can still chat or whisper when they're online – there's a bonding process in both being honest enough to say you're still looking for love.

You can always have a date if you want one...

It's essentially anonymous, so you can have as much fun as you like, without fear of judgement.

It's a fast way of meeting a lot of different men.

If all your girlfriends are dating or settled and you have no one to go out with as a singleton, it's a great way to meet people on your own.

If you've just moved to an area or hardly know anyone locally, it can help ease you into the social scene.

Cons

Men are often not what they seem – their photos may be several years out of date or not them at all.

Some of the men are actually women or groups of women having a laugh at your expense.

Men's own descriptions of themselves vary wildly from the modest but gorgeous guy who describes himself as 'of average build' and 'quite good looking' to the (sadly) more common, overweight, frog-eyed horror, who'describes himself as 'athletic and stunning'!

It's an easy playground for married men looking for some extra-marital fun – some are honest, others not.

You may get into conversation with someone who seems divine, only to find out that they live thousands of miles away from you.

Some men go from 0–60 in five 'whispers' – they start out in a friendly and chatty manner, then immediately progress to how they want to shag you on the kitchen table.

Some guys just can't type, so you'll have to put up with a lot of bizarre spellings. There's usually no spell check on internet dating sites.

Some of the longer messages are clearly from cut 'n' paste merchants and are impersonal, standard and often dull approaches.

Guys might not want to actually meet you, preferring the anonymity, safety and fantasy of virtual dating to the real thing.

There are a lot of women out there – some men, especially the more attractive guys, go into a feeding frenzy of dates so you are unlikely to be the only one that they are wooing/seeing.

Some men are just after sex, whatever they might say – but hey, no change there then!

Personal Ads

The basics

We've all seen them – those small ads in the back of the local rag or the nationals. A profile squeezed into just a few words and some choice acronyms to get maximum value for money. GSOH (Good Sense of Humour) is a favourite, though it always looks like GOSH to me! Anyway who's going to 'fess up to a BSOH...

The trouble is that a lot of these ads have a bit of a reputation as a joke – frequented by gays, marrieds, fetishists and BDSM merchants. And yet I have at least two sets of friends, and they are definitely not cross-dressing, sado-masochistic dwarves from Canvey Island, who have actually got married as a result of placing or responding to these small ads! So while some of us may sneer at them, they clearly can work. One of the big advantages of meeting a guy this way is that it by-passes the cheesy chat up line scenario of the local bar.

However, unless you choose a reputable magazine or newspaper it might be better, in the first instance, to respond to – rather than place – an ad, just to be on the safe side. As with internet dating, you must follow some of the basic safety guidelines that I've laid down, and if you do consider placing an advert – or replying to one – do be wary of where you look. In a lot of local papers, the personal ads are squeezed in between second-hand cots and used cars, and like these items, the men do not come with guarantees that they are not also soiled goods which fail all safety standards. In contrast, with papers where there are dedicated personal ad pages, you will often get a voicemail box, which will allow you to listen to someone's voice and judge their humour before agreeing to meet them.

Dating events

There has been a trend recently for big organized dating events for singles of 25 plus. With more than seven million singles in the UK alone, there's clearly a huge potential market. Since starting in London, these events are now spreading to other cities throughout the UK, and further afield. They are advertised in the local press and radio and a number are linked to websites where you can send messages to possible datees both before and after the main event.

Although they are a bit on the pricey side, these events are a great night out for singles offering a wealth of attractions on the night. These might include a clubbing area, salsa dancing lessons, speed dating, astro-dating, a chill-out room, an area for soundbite talks on subjects such as flirting and

Reading between the lines

Apply the same rules that you would when reading the hyperbole used by estate agents, such as 'compact and bijou' = 'minute' and 'potential for the DIY expert' = total wreck. Here is a basic translation guide:

Professional = got a job
Creative = hasn't got a job
TLC (Tender Loving Care) = mummy's boy
Romantic = soppy
Gentle = a wuss
Sensitive = shy
Old-fashioned = dull
Looks unimportant = a virgin and desperate
ACA (All Calls Answered) = seriously desperate
LTR (Long-term relationship) = never had a relationship that lasted beyond the weekend
Fun-loving = looking for a shag
Sexy = ditto

Passionate = looking for lots of shags
Nights in = looking for a shag, but mean with it
Open-minded = looking for a shag in rubber
Very Good Looking = vain
Laid back = lazy
Easy-going = ditto
Free-spirited = does drugs
Spiritual = wants to do drugs with you
Highly sociable = drinks heavily
Well-built = fat
Cuddly = obese
Animal loving = doesn't get out much

body language plus a representative from an internet or conventional dating agency. Icebreaker games, text dating and a whole host of other match-making devices conspire to create an evening of fun and chaos with ample opportunity to meet the maximum number of potential mates in the shortest possible time. With up to 1500 singles attending per night, it is clearly a highly lucrative business for the organizers. The first drink is usually free, although thereafter you have to pay over-inflated prices for food and drink, but the atmosphere is terrific and there's certainly no shortage of upwardly mobile singles all looking for a date. And it's a measure of just how far we've come in terms of stigma-free singledom, that one such event was recently billed as 'The Desperate and Dateless Ball', but was chock full of glamorous, good-looking and seemingly far from desperate singles all looking for a good time. At the time of printing, Chemistry is the leading dating-event organizer. At present, they are only operating only in London, but surely it's only a matter of time before these events become country-wide.

Speed Dating

Speed dating was imported form the US, where it's been a huge success. Based on the key ingredients for chemistry and attraction – voice, humour and looks, it works roughly like this:

❶ Anything from 10 to 30 women and men meet at an agreed location.

❷ You are paired off at tables for two and given approximately three minutes to chat and get to know each other.

❸ You are each given a card to keep track of the people that you meet and to decide whether you would like to meet with them again.

❹ After three minutes a bell or a buzzer goes, or music is played, signalling that the guy has to move to the next table while another one comes to yours.

❺ You discreetly mark your card as to whether you'd like to see him again – the guy does this too, but it's harder for him, as he has to keep moving on.

❻ As well as a break or two – depending on how many people are there – the three-minute process repeats until all the couples have met each other.

❼ There's usually a chance to relax and mingle at the end of the evening.

❽ You then hand your card in and if two of you have both 'ticked' each other, email addresses will be swapped care of the organizers and further contact can be made.

Clinical? Yes, but is a good shortcut to meeting people and it saves spending hours with someone on a date, when you know from the first few minutes that there's no chance that a relationship could develop. Looks, humour, character and voice are instrumental in knowing whether there's chemistry there and while speed dating can't give any guarantees – any more than any other kind of 'arranged' dating – it's certainly a start. And if you sat down, took one look, listened for a moment and thought 'no way' it's a hell of a time- saver before you have to make your excuses and go home. I've tried it and think it's definitely fun, though probably not for the shyer or more tongue-tied person, as the pressure is definitely on to meet and greet in a pretty short space of time. It's definitely worth having a drink first, just to loosen up.

Speed Dating Tips

@ Smile – always a great start and a good icebreaker.

@ Welcome the guy to your table – even if he looks like the creature time forgot, it will make him feel at ease.

@ Hold your head up and make eye contact. It shows openness and confidence.

@ Try an unusual question. 'What would your best mate say if he knew you were here?' or 'What's a nice guy like you doing in a place like this?' It might be corny but it's a lot better than the 'where do you live?' or 'what do you do for a living?' that he's heard several times already and it establishes that you have a dry sense of humour that he may or may not respond favourably to.

@ Wear a little discreet scent. It'll help mellow the moment.

@ Look smart and sassy, but avoid too much cleavage spillage. He's there to talk to you, not your tits.

Email

The advent of email has had a liberating effect on the singles scene. Whereas you might never consider actually calling a guy to ask for a date, somehow typing a witty line or two with a suggestion that a drink sometime might be fun, seems much more harmless and less bold. It's also a great way to say thanks for the first date and maybe he fancies coming with you to a girlfriend's party next weekend?

Emailing can be done discreetly at work and it's a great icebreaker. You can send a joke that you've just received or chat without actually going into the next date scenario. It's also ideal, of course, for keeping in contact with someone when they've moved to the other side of the world or just a branch office. While I'm a firm believer that the ease of email has had a massively liberating effect on dating, it must be used wisely. It is not acceptable to dump someone by email for example. That must be done face to face, as I said previously (see page 145). Bombarding someone with emails – which is just email stalking in effect – is also a definite no-no.

Email has also developed it's own language – just like internet 'whispers' and text messaging – and these are called emoticons. We all know the smiley face : -), but there's a whole range of emoticons that can be used to enhance and personalize what is essentially an impersonal method of communication.

Here is a handy list of the most common emoticons:

: >	Smiling	: ~ (	Crying
; D	Laughing	: <>	A yawn
: *	A kiss	O; >	Angel (used for
;)	A wink		'innocent' remarks)
: (	Sad face	}; >	Devil (used for
: X	My lips are sealed		'naughty' remarks)
: I	I am not amused	@>—`—-`—-	A rose
: o	Surprise		

Mobile phones

This is another great dating add-on that has completely done away with the unpleasantness of hanging around at home wondering if 'he' is going to ring. You can now go out, wherever you want, and providing you've remembered to recharge the battery, you can wait for your call Martini style – any time, any place, anywhere…

Because a mobile phone is so portable and personal, it is often preferable to give out your mobile number rather than your landline or work number. It also has the advantage of coming with it's own caller display so that you can choose whether or not you want to answer it. If you don't take the call you'll still get a voicemail or at least a call record (if he doesn't choose to leave a message). You can also choose to permanently disguise your number when calling from mobile to mobile, but that's always struck me as a bit sad… And of course you can always send text messages from your mobile phone.

Text appeal

Text messaging was originally devised as a business communication tool, SMS (short message service) as it is technically known, but it has come a long way since then. We now send 50 million text messages a day world-wide, and over 20 per cent of us have used text messaging to ask someone out on a date! Unsurprisingly, there is a significant increase in texting in the UK between 10pm and 2am on Friday and Saturday nights – key dating time.

Like email, it is a fantastic – yet non-intrusive way – of keeping in contact with a new date. A simple 'thanks for the evening: safe journey home' is a great way to end an evening. It says: 'I wouldn't dream of ringing you, just in case you didn't have a great time and don't want to see me again, but I want you to know that I did have a great time and would like another date.'

It's also a discreet way of keeping in touch right through a relationship and you can be witty, flirtatious, sexy, or just let someone know what time the movie starts – whatever takes your fancy. It develops its own rules of engagement over time. Leaving a reply for a few days might show a waning interest, whereas a swift response shows he's definitely keen. Text messaging can even take on a life of it's own once you've had a few drinks. Somehow the temptation to text when you know you really shouldn't, can become overwhelming after a night out with the girls. And sometimes, you've just got to stop yourself. The 'treat 'em mean, keep 'em keen' kind of strategy you've kept up so well, can all fall apart with a drunken and slushy text that you might never have sent when sober. Tipsy texts are generally not a good idea, unless you're both definitely up for it. Texting is also like slipping a note to the boy you fancied at school – it's still just a little bit surreptitious, fun and secret.

Basically, text messaging means that you can contact someone without worrying where they are or what they're doing. It avoids that wall of silence that comes with being out of range, in a business meeting or at a noisy bar. And it avoids that irritating cliché – 'I'm on the train'… Just be careful that texting doesn't become so addictive that you miss out on the pleasures of a person to person phone call – it's an easy habit to fall into. However most phones only have the space to give you 160-character messages – including the spaces between words – and anyway they're supposed to be short and to the point, that's half the fun. As a result 'txt msg' abbreviations have become more popular over the last few years – mainly amongst teenagers. Here are just a few of them, all in 'shouting' caps for simplicity:

AKA	Also known as	G2G	Got to go
ASAP	As soon as possible	GMTA	Great minds think
A/S/L	Age, sex, location		alike
B4	Before	GR8	Great
B4N	Bye for now	HAGN	Have a good night
BCNU	Be seeing you	HAGO	Have a good one
BTW	By the way	HF	Have fun
CM	Call me	HOT4U	Hot for you
CUL8R	See you later	IG2R	I've got to run
CW2CU	Can't wait to see you	ILU	I love you
CWYL	Chat with you later	ILY	I love you
CYA	See ya	JK	Just kidding
DEGT	Don't even go there	KISS	Keep it simple, stupid
F2F	Face to face	KIT	Keep in touch

L8R	Later	2NITE	Tonight
N1	Nice one!	2L8	Too late
RUF2T	Are you free to talk?	TU	Thank you
SPST	Same place, same time	LMAO	Laughing my arse off
		LOL	Laughing out loud
SOTMG	Short of time, must go	LTNS	Long time, no see
		MUSM	Miss you so much
SRY	Sorry	NRN	No response necessary
SUL	See you later		
SUP	What's up?	OO	Over and out
TC	Take care	OMG	Oh my god
TGIF	Thank god it's Friday	PLZ	Please
TMI	Too much information	TY	Thank you
TTFN	Ta-ta for now	WAN2TLK	Want to talk?
T2GO	Time to go	WKD	Weekend
TTYL	Talk to you later	WTF	What the fuck?
TTYS	Talk to you soon	XOXOX	Hugs and kisses
2MORO	Tomorrow		

further information

websites to visit and books to read

USEFUL WEBSITES

There are a huge number of Websites out there in the cyber world, just waiting to match you up with the perfect partner or offer advice. These are some of my personal favourites.

Relationship Advice
www.handbag.com
www.ivillage.co.uk
www.ivillage.com
www.DrDating.com
www.flirtzone.com
www.thedatingdoctor.com
www.nomeancity.org

Internet Dating
www.Udate.com
www.DatingDirect.com
www.Match.com
www.Kiss.com
www.LoveandFriends.com
www.Gorgeousboyfriends.com

Dating Events
www.chemistryevent.com
www.thesinglesolution.com

Speed Dating
www.speedater.co.uk
www.ukspeeddating.com

Introduction Agencies
www.sara-eden.co.uk
www.drawingdownthemoon.co.uk
www.onlylunch.co.uk
www.clubsirius.com

For the boys
These sites are designed for men, but they make revealing reading!

www.askmen.com
www.getgirls.com

FURTHER READING

The Single Life
Celebrating Single: Living on Your Own and Liking It, Joan Allen (Capital Books, 2001)
The Girl Code: The Secret Language of Single Women, Diane Farr (Little Brown, 2001)
The Improvised Woman: Single Women Reinventing Single Life, Marcelle Clements (Norton, 1999)

Expectations
Bad Girl's Guide to Getting What you Want, Cameron Tuttle (Chronicle, 2000)
The Little Book of Getting What you Want, John Gray (Vermillion, 2001)
Men are from Mars, Women are from Venus, John Gray (HarperCollins 2002)

Self-confidence and Self-esteem
Fear Busting: A 10 Step Plan That Will Change Your Life, Pete Cohen (HarperCollins, 2003)
Feel the Fear and Do it Anyway, Susan Jeffers (Rider, 1997)
Increasing Confidence, Philippa Davies (Dorling Kindersley, 2003)
Men Like Women Who Like Themselves, Steven Carter and Julia Sokol (Bantam Doubleday Dell, 1997)
Super Confidence: The Woman's Guide to Getting What You Want Out of Life, Gael Lindenfield (HarperCollins, 1989)
The Break-up Survival Kit: Emotional Rescue for the Newly Single, Dr Pam Spurr (Robson, 2001)

Compatibility
Date…or Soul Mate?: How to Know if Someone is Worth Pursuing in Two Dates or Less, Neil Clark Warren (Thomas Nelson, 2002)
Should We Stay Together: The Compatibility Test, Jeffrey H. Larson (Jossey Bass Wiley, 2000)

Flirt Mode
The Fine Art of Flirting, Joyce Jillson (Simon & Schuster, 1986)
The Little Book of Flirting, Peta Heskell (HarperCollins, 2002)
Flirt Coach, Peta Heskell (HarperCollins, 2001)

Body Language

Body Language, Allan Pease (Sheldon Press, 1997)
Body Language Secrets: Read the Signals and Find Love, Wealth and Happiness, Susan Quilliam (HarperCollins, 1997)
The Secrets of Sexual Body Language, Martin Lloyd-Elliott (Ulysses Press, 2001)

Dating

Flirt Coach, Peta Heskell (HarperCollins, 2001)
The Real Rules: The Ultimate Dating Makeover, Barbara De Angelis (Island Books, 1997)
Would Like to Meet…, Tracey Cox, Jeremy Milnes and Jay Hunt (BBC Books, 2002)

Relationships

Hot Relationships: How to Have One, Tracey Cox (Corgi, 2000)
Why Men Don't Listen and Women Can't Read Maps, Allan and Barbara Pease (Orion, 2001)

Techno-dating

Speed Dating: The Smarter, Faster Way to Lasting Love, Sue Deyo (HarperCollins, 2002)
Virtual Foreplay: Finding your Soulmate Online, Eve Heschner Hogan (Hunter House, 2001)

Sex

Come Hither! A Commonsense Guide to Kinky Sex, Gloria Brame (Fusion Press, 2001)
The Guide to Getting it On!, Paul Joannides (Vermilion, 2001)
Hot Sex, Tracey Cox (Corgi, 1999)
Sex Positions: Over 100 Truly Explosive Tips, Lisa Sussman (Carlton, 2001)
Supersex, Tracey Cox (Dorling Kindersley, 2002)
Women's Pleasure or How to Have an Orgasm as Often as You Want, Rachel Swift (Pan, 1994)

INDEX